High Holiday HIGHLIGHTS
Make Them Your Spiritual Adventure

Other Books by the Author:

Add Life to Your Years
From Heart to Heart
From Week to Week
Judaism Meets the Challenge
Judaism Looks at Life

Coedited with Rabbi Morris Silverman:

Prayer Book for Summer Camps
Tisha B'av Services
Selihot: Prayers for Forgiveness

High Holiday HIGHLIGHTS
Make Them Your Spiritual Adventure

By

Rabbi Hillel E. Silverman

Ktav Publishing House
Brooklyn, NY

Copyright © 2003 Hillel E. Silverman

Library of Congress Cataloging-in-Publication Data

Silverman, Hillel E., 1924-
  High Holiday highlights : make them your spiritual adventure / by Hillel E. Silverman.
    p. cm.
  ISBN 0-88125-816-4
  1. High Holidays—Liturgy. 2. High Holidays—Anecdotes. 3. Exempla, Jewish. I. Title.
  BM693.H5S65 2003
  296.4'31—dc22
                                                    2003015019

Published by
Ktav Publishing House
527 Empire Blvd.
Brooklyn, NY 11225
www.ktav.com | orders@ktav.com
(718) 972-5449

CONTENTS

Foreword	vii
1. Stories and Anecdotes To Introduce Prayers	1
3. Rosh ha-Shanah Eve	35
4. Rosh ha-Shanah	45
5. *Kol Nidrei*	81
6. Yom Kippur	115
7. *Yizkor* of Yom Kippur	131
8. *Ne'ilah*	139

**TO OUR PARENTS
IN GRATITUDE FOR
THEIR INSPIRATION**

**Dr. Emanuel and Gertrude Sigoloff
Rabbi Morris and Althea Silverman**

FOREWORD

Nothing in Judaism compares to the spirituality, excitement, and profundity of the High Holiday experience. Jews, oftentimes far removed from their religious identity and commitment, are drawn as if by a magnet to Rosh ha-Shanah and Yom Kippur. However, attendance at these services is a mere perfunctory rite of family nostalgia unless we prepare ourselves to enter this spiritual adventure through study and understanding. The High Holiday experience must come alive as an impetus to individual growth, heightened moral sensitivity, and worthwhile achievement during the coming year.

This is the goal of *High Holiday Highlights: Make Them Your Spiritual Adventure.*

I have compiled introductions to prayers, explanations of traditions, stories, and anecdotes that I have presented from the pulpit on the High Holidays during the last fifty years as a rabbi.

This book is not only a source for rabbis for their conducting of High Holiday services, but also for the thinking and sensitive layperson who wants to come away from the spiritual adventure of the High Holiday experience with a more profound perception of the values and insights of Jewish tradition. The High Holiday experience can enhance and enrich our personal lives and day-to-day relationships.

The first chapter contains stories and anecdotes that serve as introductions to the spiritual themes and messages of the High Holiday liturgy and traditions. For the rabbi, many could be developed into sermons appropriate for the occasion.

In succeeding chapters, the introductions to some of the prayers that are duplicated on Rosh ha-Shanah and Yom Kippur can be used when appropriate (e.g., *U-netanneh tokef, Kaddish, Amidah*). Prayers repeated on Kol Nidrei and Yom Kippur can be selected for one or the other (e.g., *Shema kolenu*, the confessional).

A careful perusal of this book will highlight your High Holidays and enhance your spiritual adventure in the years to come.

I express deepest gratitude to my colleagues Rabbi Mitchell M. Hurvitz and Dr. Shelley M. Buxbaum for their assistance and suggestions and to my wife Roberta for her support and encouragement.

CHAPTER 1

STORIES AND ANECDOTES TO INTRODUCE PRAYERS

COUNT YOUR CHANGE BEFORE LEAVING

I once met someone whom I had not seen in several years. After a big hello and an exchange of greetings about family, friends, and health, he said to me, "You look great! You have not changed a bit!"

After we parted, I thought about his statement, "I have not changed a bit." I suppose he meant it to be a compliment. He implied that since he had last seen me, my hair was not any grayer, I had not put on too much weight, and that I seemed to be in good shape. I had not changed a bit! He meant it as a compliment, and I took it as such.

On Rosh ha-Shanah, I wonder if "You haven't changed a bit" is a compliment. How does God see us today compared to last year? He would probably say to many of us, "You are in bad shape. You have not changed a bit since last year!"

Near the cash register of many stores is a large sign that reads: "Count Your Change Before Leaving." I think this reminder applies not only to cash. "Count your change" is good spiritual advice as well. Each of us should be able to list and count the ways in which we have changed, preferably for the better, since last Rosh ha-Shanah.

As we approach the New Year, let us count our change before leaving synagogue. Let us make sure that when God sees us, He will say, "You look great! You have changed a lot since last year!" Then, we can look forward to a New Year marked by further growth and greater understanding, a year in which we will be deserving of God's blessings of contentment, good health, and *naḥat* for our families and ourselves.

CHARITY

A miser bet ten dollars on the lottery every day. Finally, he won, and the prize was ten million dollars!

His wife was worried about how to break the news to him, for she knew that he had a heart condition. She went to the rabbi and asked him to tell her husband the news. However, she warned him to be careful because of her husband's heart condition. She told him to talk about the weather, to talk about sports, and then, gradually, work the topic around to the lottery.

This is what the rabbi did. He talked about sports. He talked about the weather. Then he said, "Tell me, Jake, I hear that you play the lottery. Is that true?"

"Yep," said the man, "every single day."

"How much do you play for?" asked the rabbi.

"Ten dollars every single day," said the man.

"Tell me, Jake, what would you do if you won ten million dollars?" asked the rabbi.

"I would give it all to the *shul*," said the man.

The rabbi had a heart attack!

COMMUNICATION

The story is told of a husband who was standing at the grave of his recently deceased wife. When the funeral was finished, the rabbi gently prodded him to "move on." Three times the rabbi urged him to leave, but the husband refused. He exclaimed, "You don't understand, I love my wife."

The rabbi placed his arm around him and said, "I know, I understand; but it is now time to leave the cemetery."

The husband tearfully exclaimed, "I love my wife, and I finally almost told her."

Rosh ha-Shanah and Yom Kippur urge us to communicate to each other what we feel in our heart, how much we care, and how much our loved ones mean to us.

GRATITUDE

A customer once entered a department store and was greeted with a band, applause, and television coverage.

"You are the millionth customer to enter our store, and we will reward you with a number of prizes!"

Later, she was asked by the store manager, "What did you come into our store to buy?" The customer was chagrined, "I came to file a complaint!'

How easy it is to complain and find fault.

Another story concerns a little boy who was dragged to sea but rescued by the lifeguard. His grandmother, standing by the shore, prayed that he would be rescued. When her little grandson was brought to shore, she exclaimed, "He had a hat on his head!"

A MULTIFACETED PEOPLE

Shortly after he received the Nobel Prize, I. B. Singer told a story about a Jewish man who had gone to Vilna for his first visit. When he came back, he said to a friend, "The Jews of Vilna are a remarkable people. I saw a Jew who studied all day long, the Talmud. I saw a Jew who all day long was scheming to get rich. I saw a Jew who was always raising the red flag, calling for revolution. I saw a Jew who was running after every woman. I saw a Jew who was an ascetic and avoided women."

The other man said, "I don't know why you're so astonished. Vilna is a big city, and there are many Jews, of all types."

"No," said the first man, "It was the same Jew."

SELF-INVENTORY

A young man walked into a drug store to make a telephone call. He left the door of the booth open, and the storekeeper could not help overhearing the conversation. The young man was apparently talking to the manager of a firm asking him whether a certain position was filled, and the answer was in the affirmative. He then proceeded to ask whether the new employee was satisfactory. To this, too, the answer was apparently yes. The call was finished and the young man, with a look of contentment on his face, sat down at the fountain to have a drink. The manager came and, after apologizing for his unintentional eavesdropping, asked him whether he was interested in a job. The young man said, "No, thank you, I have a job."

"Then why did you inquire about the position on the phone?" asked the storekeeper.

"Oh, that was my job, I was just checking up on myself."

Subjecting one's performance on Rosh ha-Shanah to a periodic self-evaluation is an important, if rare, exercise and an antidote to the smug self-righteousness that embraces most people.

FUTILITY

There was an article in the newspaper about a grandmother who crossed the Atlantic every day, landed in London, and then returned a few hours later to New York. This cost her many hundreds of thousands of dollars a year. Her grandson was asked, "Why does your grandmother do this?"

He answered, "My grandmother likes to fly!"

For many, life can be likened to this futile activity of the grandmother. We live in frenzy; our activities have no purpose; we cater to our whims and fancy.

THE DAY OF JUDGMENT

Rabbi Levi Isaac of Berdichev once heard a cobbler passing his window exclaiming, "Do you have anything to repair?"

The rabbi cried out in reply, "This is *Yom ha-Din* (i.e., the Day of Judgment), and I have not as yet prepared my soul."

THE UNKNOWN

The High Holidays instruct us that we can determine what we make of our lives. We have limited control of our health. Accidents, misfortune, and acts of nature can destroy us. Nothing is more frightening than the unknown. We cannot determine what happens to us, but we can control our reaction to these happenings.

Viktor Frankl wrote, "Man's freedom is not freedom from conditions, but rather freedom to take a stand on whatever conditions might confront us."

VALUES

Guy de Maupassant wrote a story about a poor housemaid who took a necklace from her wealthy employee to wear to a dance. She lost the necklace and borrowed money to replace it so that her employer would not realize what had happened.

For the rest of her life, she worked and struggled to repay this debt. Years later, she met her employer and told her the truth.

Her employer exclaimed, "How foolish. It was false! Just an imitation!" Oftentimes, our values, goals, and strivings are false and just imitations.

BEST IN OURSELVES

Rabbi Zusya of Hanipoli, before his death, wept and said, "In the coming world, God will not ask, 'Why were you not Isaiah?' "

"Then why do you weep?" asked his disciples.

"Because God will ask me, 'Why were you not Zusya?' Have I lived up to the best in me? What shall I answer?"

Professor Mordecai Kaplan uses the phrase, "We must be fully human," meaning, we must live to our fullest potential and achieve the very best of our capabilities.

IN TIME OF HAPPINESS

Rabbi Bunam once said that everyone must have two pockets. In the right pocket is the inscription, "For my sake the world was created." In the left pocket there is the inscription, "I am but dust and ashes."

When one is depressed, unhappy, and miserable, he should read the inscription in his right pocket, "For my sake the world was created."

When one is proud and indulges in self-aggrandizement, he should remove the quotation from his left pocket, "I am but dust and ashes!"

WINDOWS TO THE SOUL

Rabbi David Wolpe comments that the Talmud teaches that one should not pray in a room without windows. According to Rav Kook, this is because prayer without recognition of the outside world, one's responsibilities and duties, is empty. Why would one choose to pray to God in a cramped, narrow corner, unrelated to the vast panorama of God's world.

The Talmud may also be making the reverse point—not that we look out, but that others must look in. To see someone lift his heart to God can be heartening. Knowing devotion exists can kindle our own devotion. Although we cannot be sure what goes on in another's heart (as Queen Elizabeth I famously commented in her declaration of religious tolerance, "I seek not to carve windows into men's souls."), we can watch others pray and be inspired.

The Ba'al Shem Tov taught that when you see someone sway in prayer not to think it strange. Compare it to a man passing by a glass house where inside, people are dancing. Since he cannot hear the music, he sees only the strange rhythms. The music may be playing, even though we cannot hear it.

How do we know? That is why we have windows.

TEMPTATION

A New York City couple received through the mail two tickets to a smash Broadway hit. Oddly, the gift arrived without a note, and they wondered who had sent it. On the night of the performance, they dressed formally, attended the show, had a night on the town, and returned home in the wee hours.

When they entered their condominium, they discovered that their home had been ransacked. Valuable furs, jewels, and electronics were missing. On the pillow was this simple note: "Now you know where the tickets came from."

It was a nameless thief, a burglar masquerading as a benefactor, a second-story man disguised as a friend.

All these images describe the sins to which we are prone—habits that help us to cope but outrage others, good intentions meant to assist but alienate people, behaviors that seem to give us pleasure but end up causing us pain.

Let us not fall for it this year. The thief is not going to trick us this time. Next year, let us say with a well-known professional basketball player for the Dallas Mavericks, who sat out for three years while battling drug addiction, "I may not be the person I want to be, but thank God I'm not the person I used to be."

REPENTANCE

A Protestant minister once said, "There are four ways you can act when you have done something wrong. You can curse, nurse, rehearse, or reverse. You can curse your action, and blame others for your improper acts and decisions. You can nurse your errors, and keep doing what you were previously doing and merely indulge in self-pity. You can rehearse your errors, and repeat them but do nothing to change them. However, you also can reverse your actions, and you can change your way of life.

In the area of family relations, many of us have been underachievers. We can change. Will we?

PRIORITIES

When Paul Tsongas resigned from the United States Senate because of illness, he noted that among the many letters that he had received, one especially had moved him: "No one on his death bed," his correspondent advised, "ever said, 'I wish I had spent more time at my business.'"

CHARITY

A miser came to a ḥasidic rebbe to ask for a blessing. "Look out the window," said the rebbe. "What do you see?"

"I see men, women, and children," answered the miser.

"Now look into the mirror. What do you see?" asked the rebbe.

"I see only myself," answered the miser.

The difference between a window and a mirror is a coating of silver. If you do not part with your silver, you will never see anyone else but yourself. Break your mirror and receive seven years of *mazal*.

HEARING BUT NOT LISTENING

Paul Simon wrote a fascinating song titled "The Sounds of Silence" that frighteningly captures a truth of our society: "People talking without speaking / people hearing without listening." A member of my synagogue told me of an encounter between his father and a rabbi acquaintance of his.

"How are you?" politely inquired the rabbi.

"My wife died two weeks ago," responded the gentleman.

"That's nice. And how is business?" continued the rabbi, who obviously had asked his second question before listening to the answer to his first.

So ingrained within our social fabric is this habit of not listening that Emily Post insists that the only proper answer to the question, "How are you?" is, "How are you?" because people rarely listen to how you really are. Indeed, it is commonplace to notice that while in the midst of making a point to a friend, the friend is already formulating his response—without really listening to what you are trying to say. It is probably because of the popular music that is so loud—we do not listen to one another anyway, so we might as well drown out any conversation. Moreover, if you are accustomed to not listening to others, you stop listening to yourself as well.

SELF-RIGHTEOUSNESS

The religious life is a never-ending struggle. Whoever thinks he has conquered pride, sin, and temptation forever only deceives himself. A ḥasidic teacher once commented that the Satan is very clever. Before we do a good deed, he tries to talk us out of it. He says it is cold outside; why get up, why bother? If he fails, and we do the good deed, he comes from behind and pats us on the back, and says, "See how pious you are!"

The second ploy of the Satan is as dangerous as the first.

A SPIRITUAL CHECK-UP

In New York, there is a compulsory car inspection law. Every automobile must be checked once a year. This is a good law because it makes our cars safer. On another level, more people make it a practice to have an annual medical check-up. Perhaps some day, a law will be passed to make an annual physical check-up mandatory, too. Rosh ha-Shanah is reserved for the Jew to have a spiritual check-up. We want to know how we are doing Jewishly. Are we living useful lives? Do our lives have Jewish significance? Rosh ha-Shanah is, in a sense, the annual general meeting of the Jewish people, at which the chairperson who directs our fortunes is reconfirmed in office.

A SMALL *TALLIT*

A woman came to a Jewish bookstore to purchase a *tallit* for her husband. She rejected the first one the proprietor showed her saying, "It is too expensive and too large; I want something smaller."

He showed her a smaller one. She rejected it as well. This went on for some time. The bookseller became impatient. Finally, he said to her, "Lady, is your husband a midget?"

"Oh, no. My husband is six feet tall. But, you see, for the one time a year that he will use it, the smallest *tallit* you have will be big enough."

We speak of buying or possessing a *siddur*, a *Kiddush* cup, a *tallit*, or candlesticks. How can we truly possess these religious items when we do not *daven*, when we do not make *Kiddush*, when we do not *bentshen licht*?

THERE IS A GOD

The story is told of Rabbi Levi Isaac of Berdichev that he once summoned all the Jews of Berdichev to assemble in the town square the following day at noon, because he had an important announcement to make. Merchants were to close their shops, nursing mothers to bring their infants; everyone was to be there. People wondered what the important announcement could be. An imminent pogrom? A new tax? Could it be that the rabbi was leaving? or perhaps seriously ill? At noon, before the entire community, he rose and said, "I,

Levi Isaac, son of Sarah, have gathered here to tell you that there is a God!"

If there is a God, our lives are redeemed from meaninglessness, because our choices and our actions matter to God. If there is a God, there are things that we will be tempted to do but will refrain from, because we understand that they are wrong. If there is a God, we will not be afraid to spend our limited amount of love and compassion, because we will know that God will be there to replenish us when we run out. If we believe that there is a God, we will treat one another more kindly, because we will recognize the image of God in our neighbor, whatever his race, religion, mental ability, or earning capacity.

A REWARD FOR PIETY

A father was personally supervising the packing of his son's *tallit* and *tefillin* as the youth was preparing to leave his childhood home for an out-of-town college. Foreseeing possible financial stress, the father surreptitiously slid a substantial sum into his son's *tefillin* bag. It was not long before the boy exhausted his funds and sent a frantic plea for financial aid. Instead of money, he received the following cryptic message: "Pray to God, from whom cometh all help." Exasperated, the boy sent a second request, emphasizing the urgency of his need. His answer was the same suggestion that he pray for assistance in his morning prayers. Finally, seeing no alternative, the boy heeded his father's counsel. He realized that in the problems and tensions of his present life, he had neglected his morning devotions. Of course, as he donned his *tallit* and *tefillin*, he came upon the hidden hoard and understood.

There are no material rewards for pious performance. However, in a profounder sense, there are ample spiritual treasures in the performance of *mitzvot*, and one's resources are immeasurably augmented when we associate with the Divine.

THE REVIVAL OF HEBREW

St. John, in his book *The Tongue of the Prophets*, which is a fictionalized biography of Eliezer Ben-Yehuda, the father of modern Hebrew, records the following scene:

> One day when Eliezer Ben-Yehuda and his wife, Deborah, were walking down the narrow streets of Jerusalem and talking in Hebrew, a man stopped them. Tugging at the journalist's sleeve, he asked in Yiddish, "Excuse me, sir, that language you two talk, what is it?"
> "Hebrew," Ben-Yehuda replied.
> "Hebrew! People don't talk Hebrew. It is a dead language!"
> "You are wrong, my friend," Eliezer replied with a frown. "I am alive. My wife is alive. We speak Hebrew. Therefore, Hebrew is alive."

We Jews are alive today in the world. We are alive in the synagogue. We should be alive to the possibilities of all that we can do to rescue, redeem, and reaffirm Jewish life here in America and throughout the world.

INWARD, NOT OUTWARD

A police officer rushed to a telephone booth in response to an emergency call from a woman who said that she was locked in the booth. He easily released the caller, and explained to her that the door opened inwards, not outwards.

TOUCHING UP OUR LIVES

Tolstoy tells a story of a Russian painter named Karl Bryullov, who was also an art teacher. One day, Tolstoy watched Bryullov touch up a pupil's work and it came to life. All that the painting needed was a slight correction here and there to make it into a fine work of art. Many of us need just a little "touching up" of the canvas of our life.

A U-TURN IN LIFE

In driving our cars, from time to time, we come to an intersection with a sign warning motorists: NO U-TURNS. To turn back at such a corner would obstruct traffic, and therefore all cars must go straight ahead. However, Rosh ha-Shanah tells us that we can make a u-turn in life.

SHEDDING BAD HABITS

In years gone by, ships that sailed the ocean gradually acquired a mass of barnacles, and this retarded their speed. Unless, at regular intervals, they were scraped, the usefulness of the ship was impaired. If a ship needs a periodic scraping to shed its unnecessary accumulations, how much more so is it true of human beings?

YOU CAN DO BETTER

During the Ten Days of Penitence, a ḥasidic rebbe was walking through the marketplace, and he overheard a customer bargaining with a merchant. The merchant proposed a price, and the buyer said, "You can do better than that." The shopkeeper then came up with a lower price, and the customer persisted, "You can do better than that." At this point, the rebbe lifted his eyes heavenwards and said, "Master of the Universe, isn't that the message of the *Yamim Nora'im*? Are You not saying to us, 'You can do better than that; you can do better than that'?"

SOILING OUR SOULS

A ḥasid once approached his rebbe and said, "Can you teach us the meaning of *teshuvah* as it pertains to us, since we are not a group of sinners?"

The rebbe replied, "Go to the creek on the outskirts of the town, and watch what transpires there, and then report to me."

The disciple carried out the instructions of his master, but returned baffled by the rebbe's suggestion.

"All I saw were women doing their laundry by the creek. They came with dirty garments, scrubbed them clean, and at the end of the week, they returned with more dirty garments to scrub them clean again."

The rebbe explained, "In our encounter with the world, our souls become soiled, and they must be scrubbed repeatedly. *Teshuvah* is a kind of scrubbing and cleansing that must be continuous."

THANK GOD

The wife of David Grossman, the Israeli author, gave birth to their first child at Hadassah Hospital. He was so excited on his drive back home that all the sights seemed alive and new to him. As he rounded a curve in the road, the city of Jerusalem appeared before him bathed in a sea of lights. He stopped the car and sat reflecting on both the birth of his son and the rebirth of Jerusalem. Filled with the majesty of the moment, he said to himself, "Don't be an idiot; thank God." However, as a lifelong atheist, he repressed the feeling and did not do it.

His story is reminiscent of the old couple married for fifty-eight years who were sitting on the porch in their rocking chairs. The old man looked straight at the field and suddenly broke the silence of the hour, "You know, woman, sometimes it takes everything I have within me to keep from telling you how much I love you."

FOR THE SINS WE WISH WE HAD COMMITTED

A Jew who had been away from the synagogue for most of his life tried to rediscover his Jewish roots.

He came to services on Yom Kippur. He took a front seat, and stayed all day. He did not leave. It was a very traditional service; in fact, he recited every word in the *mahzor*. In addition, he was there for the last *shofar* call and through *ma'ariv*.

When the day was done, he came to me with an expression I can only describe as incredulous. "You know something?" he said, "I've apologized for sins today that I wish I had committed!"

THE SIN OF INDIFFERENCE

A few years ago, Billings, Montana hit the headlines. During Ḥanukkah, rocks were thrown through the windows of two Jewish homes which were displaying *ḥanukkiyyot*. The citizens of that community were upset by what happened, so they held classes on prejudice and meetings to deal with the pain. Although there are only some sixty Jewish families in the city and Montana is a hotbed of hate groups, militias, and bigotry, the people of Billings decided, "Not in our town." with the result that almost every home in Billings displayed a *menorah* during all of that December in a window. A speaker at a convocation to honor the citizens suggested that Billings "just might become the Denmark of the United States." That was a touching phrase, for during World War II, of some eight thousand Jews in Denmark, only fifty perished in the Holocaust. Their fellow citizens saved the rest.

Contrast that remarkable reaction to a story that comes from the dark days of what we used to call the Cold War. At a press conference in New York City in 1969, then Soviet Premier Nikita Khrushchev received a written question, "What were you doing during all those crimes of Stalin that you have exposed and denounced?" Livid with rage, Khrushchev shouted, "Who asked that question?" Everyone remained silent. "Let him stand up!" he demanded. No one stood up. Then Khrushchev said in a lowered voice. "That's what I was doing."

However, the people of Billings felt compelled to react. They did not think they would change the world because they put *ḥanukkiyyot* in their windows. No! They did it because they had to transform themselves. That is our mission, too, and may we accomplish it during the coming year and the years ahead.

KIDDUSH HA-SHEM: **THREE GENERATIONS**

An obituary appeared in the *Jerusalem Post* after the Six-Day War. It reported that a young man by the name of Chaim Sturman was killed at the front. It gave his family background.

His grandfather, Chaim, was among the first *ḥalutzim* who came to Israel and founded En-Harod. Before the State of Israel was established, he worked on the reclamation of the Emek, which in those days was a swamp. This Chaim Sturman was killed in 1938 by a mine planted on the road by Arabs. He was forty-seven.

Chaim left a son, Moshe, who fought under the British in the Second World War. When the new state was established, he enlisted to fight for the Haganah, the Palmach. In 1948, ten years after his father was killed, he was shot at the age of twenty-six.

Moshe left a son Chaim, named for the grandfather. The grandson joined the Zahal, and was sent to Suez where he was killed at the age of twenty-three. Three Sturmans—Chaim the grandfather, Moshe the father, and Chaim the grandson—lie side by side in graves in En-Harod.

The last line of the obituary states, "Chaim Sturman left no children."

MAN'S ORIGIN IS DUST

S. Y. Agnon won the Nobel Prize. When the news was announced, all of his friends rushed to his home in Talpiyyot to say *mazzal tov*. Hundreds of reporters and photographers came, too. They filled the room to overflowing. One of the photographers said, "Please sit at your desk, and pretend you are writing something, so we can pose a picture of you that way." He sat at the desk and scribbled something on a tablet and the photographers took dozens of pictures of him posed that way. When the people finally left, someone went and looked at the tablet. Agnon had written five words, words that come from the *U-netanneh tokef*: *Adam yisodo me'afar, visofo le'afar*, "Man's origin is dust and his end is dust." Those were the words that he needed to remind himself of at that triumphant moment in his life.

BLINDERS

Two leather flaps on a horse's bridle shut out the possibility of his viewing what is transpiring on the side. He is able to be victorious in racing if he acts as if his competitors do not exist.

We often place blinders on our own eyes.

There was an article recently in the *New York Times* about a narcotics detective and his wife who discovered that their daughter was a drug addict. They were overwhelmed by the shock!

As parents, oftentimes, we do not want to believe what is transpiring with our children, not necessarily narcotics, alcohol, or delinquency. Rather, we close our eyes to their talents, lack of values, standards, and goals. Too often, we push our children mercilessly. We must accept what they are and encourage them to improve.

Not only do parents put on blinders about their children, but oftentimes husbands and wives, friends, and neighbors put on blinders. We must accept people for who they are, with basic faults and failings. Without false expectations, we must encourage and inspire.

THE JOY OF *Mitzvah*

A ḥasidic rebbe once said, "When a king is at a celebration, he is approachable to many, who otherwise would be denied admittance. So, too, it is with the Almighty; when we serve God in joy he is more approachable to us."

A good example is the Sabbath Day, which many feel is a day of prohibitions and gloom. The Sabbath is not a day of sadness. Rather, the prohibitions were instituted to experience the spirit of Sabbath—"And you shall rejoice in your festival."

All of Jewish holiday observance is to promote the *simḥah shel mitzvah*, the joy of observance. The holidays, the festivals, Ḥanukkah, Purim, the erection of a *sukkah*, affixing a *mezuzah* to the door are all aspects of religious joy.

DAVENING

I once spoke at a church and found that the microphone was faulty. One of the ushers approached me and said, "Rabbi, speak loudly. The agnostics are terrible."

The *nusaḥ* (i.e., melody of prayer) need not be loud, but oftentimes soft in its spirituality. We can be caught in the fervor of the davening.

REUNION

An old woman had just arrived from Romania. Picked up by a bus in Jerusalem, she did not have sufficient money to pay the fare; the driver said that he himself would make up the difference. Some of the passengers engaged the old woman in conversation. She related that she had immigrated to Israel that week because she was certain she would find at least one of her sons alive, from whom she had been separated years before. She was traveling from place to place in the hope that she would set eyes on them. The bus passengers, attempting to be helpful, asked where she was from, her name, and the names of her sons. When the young driver heard the name, he suddenly stopped his bus and embraced her, *Mamme! Dos bin ich!* (i.e., "Mom, that's me!") The passengers began to weep and one by one they left the bus, saying to the driver, "Never mind us. Take your mother home!"

THE ELDERLY

You say you can't do anything? Can you read? Good. Read to me. My eyes aren't what they used to be.
Can you write? Good. Write a letter or card to me. My hands are shaky.
Can you sing? Good. Help me with the words, and I'll sing along.
Can you tell me about your job? I was a nurse once myself.
Can you listen? Wonderful. I'm starved for conversation.
Can you bake a sponge cake or zucchini bread or angel biscuits or fudge? They aren't on the nursing home menu but I remember how good they used to be, and I would love to taste them once again.
Do you play checkers or dominoes or rummy? Fine, so do I but there is never anyone around here who has the time. They are understaffed around here, you know.
Do you play the violin or the flute or the piano? My hearing is poor but I can hear any kind of music. Even if I fall asleep, you'll know that I enjoyed it.
Once we were some bodies, just like you. We were businessmen and businessmen's wives, teachers, nurses, beauticians, stockbrokers, and electricians, bankers, and sheriffs—and maybe a few outlaws, too. We are not all senile—just old and needing more help than our families can give us. This home, whatever its name is, is "home" to us now, and you're a welcome guest.

Please come. The welcome mat is always out. And anything that you can do for us or with us is most appreciated.

JUDAISM MAKES SENSE

Judaism is a very logical, reasonable, and pragmatic religion.

There is little of mystery and the esoteric. We are not asked to make a "leap of faith." We do not provide our people with a catechism or creed to be recited and subscribed. One of our principle prayers is "Hear, O Israel." We are asked to love the Lord our God with all our heart and soul and might, and to love our neighbor as ourselves.

We believe in one God and therefore subscribe to the principle that humankind is one. Our golden rule is "that which is hateful to thee, do not do to your fellow man." The Ten Commandments are not the whole and substance of Judaism. They are the preamble to our Constitution, which is contained and amplified in the Talmud and *Shulḥan Arukh*. Our holidays, ceremonial, and rituals are poetic symbols expressing spiritual insights and enabling us to make our lives better, richer, and more satisfying.

RELIGION MEANS MORE TO US
AS WE GROW OLDER

The teen years and college years are times of rebellion against religion. Stimulation of college professors makes us question some of the basic principles of our tradition.

However, as we become older, marry, settle down, bring children into this world, we begin to reassess our values, we begin to find the meaning that religion and the warmth of spiritual pageantry can bring into our lives.

As we get older, we begin to ask what life is all about. What am I really accomplishing? Am I truly happy? Am I missing something in life?

Many of us turn to religion for answers to these questions.

AESTHETICS AND JUDAISM

There is an aesthetic feeling to the High Holidays; a family gathered around the table, attending services together, dipping the apple in the honey, and on Kol Nidrei night, removing the scrolls of the Torah from the Ark, and wearing the *tallit*. There is so much in Judaism that has profound aesthetic enjoyment for us; the Passover *seder*, the Hanukkah candles, the building of the *sukkah*, Shabbat, Purim, and much more.

There is so much prose in life, so much which is mundane and commonplace, that we feel the need for poetry, beauty, pageantry, warmth, and charm.

JUDAISM AND CHRISTIANITY

Now for a crash course on the similarities and differences between Judaism and Christianity. We will not discuss peripheral matters, such as holiday observance, covering the head, or Hebrew liturgy.

The basic similarities that these two religions have in common are belief in the same God, the Bible (i.e., *Tanakh*), ethics and morality, and a belief that life does not end at death. However, there are basic differences which separate the two, namely, a belief in Jesus as the Messiah, the New Testament, the concept of original sin, dichotomy of the body being evil and the soul good, ritual observance replaced by faith.

WHY DOXOLOGY?

There are four basic types of prayer in the *siddur*: petition, in which we ask, confession, in which we acknowledge our failures, gratitude, through which we evince our thanksgiving, and a final form of prayer, namely, praise.

When we come to the fourth type of prayer, we note that in our prayerbooks so many of our prayers begin, "Blessed art Thou, O Lord, our God."

Why is there so much doxology, or praise of God? When we praise God, the King of Kings, we acknowledge that there is order and purpose in the world; we know who we are and what our place is in the universe. By constant acknowledgement of God, which is the purpose of our praise, we acknowledge the source of our ethics and morality.

WHY HEBREW IN THE PRAYERBOOK?

There are many reasons why Hebrew is part of our liturgy. Hebrew is a key to our past. The Bible, our prayerbook, our commentaries, and our literature are in Hebrew. The language is a bond that binds all of us together.

In addition, Hebrew is a symbol of Jewish regeneration.

The return to Israel after two millennia of diaspora is an unprecedented miracle. However, the rejuvenation of the Hebrew language after two thousand years as a language of prayer and study of holy books is also a miracle. This is a unique story in the history of languages. Eliezer Ben-Yehuda was the first Jew in two thousand years to speak Hebrew. On the boat from Russia to Israel in the 1880s, he informed his wife that upon reaching Palestine, they would speak only Hebrew in their home. His wife replied, "But I don't know Hebrew!"

His retort was, "You will learn." Their son was the first Jew in two millennia whose native tongue was Hebrew.

There are many English words borrowed from Hebrew: amen, alphabet, balm, cherub, hallelujah, jubilee, leviathan, manna, sack, shibboleth, and so on.

Many popular titles of novels and plays are taken from the Bible: *The Grapes of Wrath*; *How Green Was My Valley*; *The Valley of Decision*; *The Voice of the Turtle*; *The Good Earth*; *The Way of All Flesh*; *The Little Foxes*; *East of Eden*; *My Son, My Son*; and so on.

It is interesting that the Yale University seal contains Hebrew. The reason is that Yale was originally a Protestant seminary in which Hebrew was taught.

When the United States became a republic, it was suggested that to facilitate a complete break from England, a new language be adapted. Some proposed Hebrew as the language of the United States. What a tremendous implication this would have been for us today. Hebrew schools would be redundant, for every Jew would understand the Hebrew of the prayerbook and the Bible.

A STRANGER ON THE BUS

A light snow was falling, and the streets were crowded with people. It was Munich. A middle-aged woman was riding a city bus home from work when storm troopers suddenly stopped the coach and began examining the identification papers of the passengers. Most were annoyed, but a few were terrified. Jews were being told to leave the bus and get into a truck around the corner.

The woman watched from her seat in the rear as the soldiers systematically worked their way down the aisle. She began to tremble, tears streaming down her face. When the man next to her noticed that she was crying, he politely asked her why.

"I don't have the papers you have. I am a Jew. They're going to take me." The man exploded with disgust. He began to curse and scream at her.

"You stupid bitch," he roared. "I can't stand being near you." The SS men asked what all the yelling was about.

"Damn her," the man shouted angrily. "My wife has forgotten her papers again! I am so fed up. She always does this!"

The soldiers laughed and moved on.

The terrified woman never saw the man again. She never even knew his name.

RECONCILIATION: JEW AND ARAB

The following is a true story of an actual event, a by-product of the reunification of Judaism.

When the Old and New Cities of Jerusalem were reunited in 1967, a recently widowed Arab woman, who had been living in Old Jerusalem since 1948, wanted to see once more the house in which she formerly lived. Now that the city was one, she searched for and found her old home. She knocked on the door of the apartment, and a Jewish widow came to the door and greeted her. The Arab woman explained that she had lived there until 1948 and wanted to look around. She was invited in and offered coffee. The Arab woman said, "When I lived here I hid some valuables. If they are still here, I will share them with you half and half."

The Jewish woman refused. "If they belonged to you and are still here, they are yours." After much discussion back and forth, they entered the bathroom, loosened the floor planks, and found a horde of gold coins. The Jewish woman said, "I shall ask the government to let you keep them." She did, and permission was granted.

The two widows visited each other repeatedly, and one day, the Arab woman told her, "You know, in the 1948 fight here, my husband and I were so frightened that we ran away to escape. We grabbed our belongings, took the children, and each fled separately. We had a three-month-old son. I thought my husband had taken him, and he thought I had. Imagine our grief when we were reunited in Old Jerusalem to find that neither of us had taken the child."

The Jewish woman turned pale, and asked the exact date. The Arab woman named the date and the hour and the Jewish widow told her, "My husband was one of the Israeli troops that entered Jerusalem. He came into this house and found a baby on the floor. He asked if he could keep the house and the baby, too. Permission was granted."

At that moment, a twenty-year-old Israeli soldier in uniform walked into the room and the Jewish woman broke down in tears. "This is your son," she cried.

This is one of those incredible tales we hear. The aftermath? The two women liked each other so much that the Jewish widow asked the Arab mother, "Look, we are both widows living alone. Our children are grown up. This house has brought you luck. You have found your son, or our son. Why don't we live together?" They do.

RECONCILIATION: FATHER AND SON

A second miraculous story concerns a broken-hearted father from the United States; his only son had become a hippie, left college the year before, and vanished without a trace. The father, visiting in Jerusalem at the Wall, wrote a prayer on a piece of paper imploring God that He should restore his son to him unharmed. As he inserted his *kvitl* in a crevice in the Wall, one of the many notes embedded there fell to the ground. He bent down to retrieve it and recognized a familiar handwriting. It was that of his lost son. On the back of the paper was scrawled, "Dear God, please let me see my dad and mom again!" The young man had also placed his address on the paper. There was a most joyous reunion because two people, father and son, had offered prayer at the Wall.

WHO AM I?

With tears streaming from her cheeks, a forty-one-year-old woman addressed more than two million Israeli television viewers and sobbed, "Who am I? What is my name? Who are my parents? Are they still alive?"

She spoke in Polish, which was translated into Hebrew. She was a Catholic from Warsaw who had just arrived in Israel with a newly found friend from Herzliyyah.

I happened to be in Israel at that time and saw this program live on a popular Israeli talk show. As I watched the incredible interview between her and the "David Letterman of Israel," I was mesmerized by the unbelievable story.

Actually, two women were interviewed. The first was Herzliyyah painter Paula Weizman. She related that when in Warsaw for an exhibition of her work, she was invited to a ceremony marking the forty-fifth anniversary of the Warsaw Ghetto. Sitting beside her was a younger woman, emotionally distraught, who kept muttering, "I'm from the ghetto! I'm from the ghetto!"

She learned from this woman that in May 1943, a Polish former lieutenant colonel had stumbled over a small parcel on the sidewalk next to the ghetto wall. He was amazed to discover a whimpering baby wrapped in rags. He picked up the "parcel" and hurried home.

When his wife took the baby girl out of the wraps, she found a piece of paper with the message, "The child's name is Anna, and her birth date is October 13, 1942. May God protect her and you who have found her."

The childless couple decided to adopt the pretty seven-month-old girl, well aware that they would be executed if discovered by the Germans. They understood that the baby's Jewish parents, facing certain death, lowered the child by a string over the ghetto wall in a desperate bid to give her a chance to live.

They raised Anna as a Catholic. Her adopted father died when she was nine. At that time, her adopted mother began to tell her of her Jewish origins. When her adopted mother died, the local Jewish community and the Joint Distribution Committee befriended Anna, only fifteen years old. She was able to complete her biology studies at Krakow University. She married a Catholic engineering student and the couple has a son, twenty-one, and a daughter, fifteen.

Now the talk-show host began to interview Anna. She was in Israel to accept the Righteous Gentile medal on behalf of her departed adoptive parents. With tears in her eyes, she addressed the television audience, "I want to know who I am. I want to know about my parents. Are they still living? Will you help me?"

The talk-show host pleaded with the viewing audience to call in if they had any clue to her identity, "Does this woman resemble any member of your family? Do you recognize any facial expressions or manner of communication? Please call the television station or write to me as soon as possible."

After the television program, the station as well as the Weizman home in Herzliyyah was flooded with calls well after midnight.

Who knows, perhaps someone will be able to identify her!

This story, in different guise, can be repeated in Israel. During the last forty years, Israel has been a haven of refuge for more than two million immigrants, many of them survivors in one way or another. Israel is the promise that tales like these never need be told again.

TAKE PLEASURE IN ANOTHER'S HAPPINESS

In a small town in Poland in which most of the Jews were poor and unlearned, and where they had to compete against each other to eke out a living, there lived one man who was widely admired for his learning, his wealth, and his piety. One day, a dozen community leaders were pleased and astonished to receive an invitation to his home: "You are invited to Reb Isaac's home next Tuesday evening at six o'clock for a dinner worthy of Paradise." They could hardly wait for Tuesday to arrive. Dinner at Reb Isaac's! A meal worthy of Paradise! They all showed up promptly at six, and they were ushered into the dining room, where the table was elegantly set with porcelain, crystal, and silver. When they were seated, a servant brought Reb Isaac a roll over which he recited the traditional blessing. The servant then set a bowl of soup before him, but none for the guests. Reb Isaac began to eat his soup, commenting, "Mmm, this is such good soup. I don't remember when I've had such tasty soup." The guests were puzzled; why were they not being served as well? When Reb Isaac finished his soup, he motioned to his servant, who cleared the dish and returned a moment later with a plate of meat and vegetables for the host, and again nothing for the guests. Reb Isaac continued eating, saying, "Oh, this is so good. You have no idea what you are missing. This is so tasty, I love it."

Finally, one of the invited guests blurted out, "Reb Isaac, I don't understand. Have you brought us here to mock us? We were invited for a dinner worthy of Paradise, but you alone get the meal and we only get to watch you enjoy it. Why are you doing this to us?"

Reb Isaac smiled. "A meal worthy of Paradise indeed. What did you think it would be? Is Paradise a famous restaurant? Is Paradise somewhere one wants to go for its fine food and wine? No, Paradise is a place where people love each other enough to take pleasure in another person's happiness. Paradise is any place where you can see your neighbor being successful and not envy him for it. Paradise is a place where people know that the truly important things in life are present in such abundance that there is plenty for everyone; we do not have to snatch them away from our neighbor. And now, if we have all learned that lesson, I'll have your dinner brought out to you."

WE WERE LIKE UNTO THEM THAT DREAM

Shortly after the Six-Day War, a man named Avshalom Greenberg was buried in Israel. During the tempestuous years of World War I, he was one of a small group of Palestinian Nili spies, who, at the risk of their lives, were providing vital information to the Allies. In the dead of night in Haifa harbor, they would courageously swim out to British ships with information procured the same day about enemy troop movements. A select few of these Nili spies embarked upon a dangerous mission to Egypt and set out on foot through the Sinai desert. All but Avshalom were almost immediately captured and tortured. Just before the Turks hanged them, they related their story about their unsuccessful journey to Egypt. For fifty years, none had ever heard of the surviving member of their party, Avshalom. Did he ever reach Egypt? Was his mission successful? What happened to him? Why did he never return to his family in Palestine?

Fifty years later, at the outbreak of the Six-Day War, during the mad dash of Israeli tanks through the parched sands of the Sinai desert to the Mitla Pass, an Israeli tank commander noticed a strange sight—in the middle of the desert, a group of date palms. After the war was ended, the Israeli commander returned to those incongruous palms and from beneath them, he disinterred the remains of Avshalom. Fifty years before, with a few dried dates in his pockets, Avshalom had set out on his suicidal mission and had succumbed to the devastating heat and burning thirst of the desert. From the dried dates in his pockets, there had miraculously sprouted these date palms.

His remains were reinterred next to the grave of Theodor Herzl in the Jerusalem military cemetery.

Never in his wildest imagination did Avshalom dream that, fifty years later, tanks of the proud and powerful independent State of Israel in full pursuit of the enemy attacker, would come upon date palms, which had germinated from his mission. This, in short, is the divine miracle that is Israel today.

In the words of the psalmist:

When the Lord brought back those that returned to Zion, we were like unto them that dream. Then was our mouth filled with laughter, and our tongue with singing. . . . They that sow in tears shall reap in joy. Though he that beareth the measure of seed goeth on his way weeping, he shall come home with joy bearing his sheaves.

CHAPTER 2
ROSH HA-SHANAH EVE

LE-SHANAH TOVAH, OR "MAY IT BE A GOOD YEAR"

Tonight, to the majestic, haunting strains of the Rosh ha-Shanah liturgy, we usher in another year.

Strange how the majority culture in this country is inclined to shape, color, and even distort our once uniquely Jewish religious vocabulary. Let me share with you just two of many examples.

We greet one another in the synagogue tonight with the salutation, "Happy New Year!" Nothing could be more spiritually remote from the traditional Rosh ha-Shanah greeting, *Shanah tovah* (i.e., "A Good Year"). "Happy New Year" has Dionysian overtones foreign to our faith and tradition. Naturally, we look forward to a year of material and emotional happiness. However, it is not fun, frivolity, pleasure, and merriment that confer genuine meaning and authentic depth to the twelve months ahead. Rather, the Jew seeks a New Year of "goodness," of worthwhile, significant, creative, and altruistic achievement. Conceivably, a year can be "happy" and yet devoid of any modicum of goodness, whereas a year of goodness brings with it its own peculiar spiritual and psychological happiness. May the twelve months ahead be a year of goodness in our homes, our offices, and our community. May we perform the good and the upright.

HIGH HOLIDAYS

Another example of false cultural metapsychology is the misnomer "High Holidays." These words should choke in our throats. How can holidays be "high" unless this is a slang term indicating the worshipper's degree of intoxication? Moreover, what, per contra, are "low holidays"? The Jewish terminology is *Yamim Nor'aim* (i.e., "Days of Awe and Reverence"). During these times of anxiety and frustration, it is with fear and trembling that we assemble in our synagogues to confront our Creator and ourselves. "High Holidays" is a vulgarism. "Days of Awe" connotes so much more.

We find it more comfortable to enunciate "Happy New Year" and "High Holidays!" However, Judaism is not meant merely to comfort the disturbed, but also to disturb the comfortable.

To everyone, "A Good New Year" and a spiritual catharsis in the approaching "Days of Awe."

MEANING OF THE HIGH HOLIDAYS

The High Holidays offer an opportunity to back away from the tensions, stresses, and anxieties of day-to-day life and to consider what life is all about.

At the beginning of the month of Elul, we begin our withdrawal from the world. By Yom Kippur, we have achieved estrangement from ordinary life. After the Day of Atonement, we re-emerge into the world with renewed understanding and vigor.

This is also a time of affirmation of membership in the Jewish people. After Yom Kippur, we return to our home and build a *sukkah*. The lesson is obvious; we must return to our home and daily tasks. We begin to build the *sukkah* because we want to make our life happy and fruitful. The message of the High Holidays is to celebrate a full relationship with God and other human beings.

ROSH HA-SHANAH AND YOM KIPPUR

Rosh ha-Shanah teaches human responsibility and divine judgment—about life and renewal. Yom Kippur is concerned with human failure and divine forgiveness—about death and renunciation. From these teachings, we may return to life purified and reinvigorated.

Rosh ha-Shanah reminds us that we are responsible for our actions. Yom Kippur teaches that despite our flawed nature and our contemplation of sin, sin and guilt can and must be removed. There are three ways to avert the evil decree—through "penitence, prayer, and good deeds."

BAREKHU ET ADONAI, OR "PRAISE THE LORD"

The Ba'al Shem Tov on one Rosh ha-Shanah evening refused to enter his synagogue to conduct services. He exclaimed, "There are too many prayers entering this synagogue and too few prayers coming out of the synagogue." Too often, we carry our prayers into the synagogue, deposit them, and forget about them. May we leave the synagogue determined to fulfill the words of our prayers. More important than the prayers we bring in are the prayers we carry out.

BAREKHU: NOT PRAYER BUT ACTION

The Ba'al Shem Tov tells us about the Jew who in the month of Elul always rushed away from services.

"Why do you do this?" asked the Ba'al Shem Tov.

"I am returning home to look at my *mahzor* (i.e., High Holidays prayerbook) to see if the prayers are in order."

Replied his rebbe, "Look to yourself and to your own character, and make certain that you are in order. The *mahzor* hasn't changed this past year, but you have changed!"

SHEMA: **HEARING BUT NOT LISTENING**

"Hear, O Israel, the Lord our God is One"

The story is told of a busy lawyer, whose father lived four hundred miles away.

He would call her on the telephone: "Please come and visit me. I'm getting older and I miss you."

She would inevitably reply, "I'm busy. I have depositions and trials. Someday, I will come to see you!"

One day on the telephone, the father said to his daughter, "May I ask you a personal question? When I pass away, will you come to my funeral?"

She was very upset. "How can you ask me this? Of course, I will attend your funeral."

He replied, "Come now, I need you now more than I will need you later."

Shema means to hear and listen.

This coming year, may we listen to the pleas of our parents and children, our husbands and wives. What are they really saying to us? What are their needs and requests of us?

ADONAI EHAD, **OR "GOD IS ONE"**

A fellow officer in the Navy told me an unforgettable story about his only son whom he cherished. This commander related that when the boy was eight years old, at a summer camp in Massachusetts, a dislodged boulder had rolled down a hill and pinned him to the earth. With almost every bone in his body broken, he was rushed to the hospital. The surgeons immediately amputated one of his crushed legs.

The finest physicians and most gifted surgeons held a consultation, called in the father, and told him, "It's no use. There is no hope. He has only a day or two—at the most, three. He cannot live and there is absolutely no hope. His body is too severely crushed!"

Nevertheless, the father had hope. He would not give up, and he remained praying by the side of his son. Not for two or three days. For five weeks, his son lay there between life and death. The doctors again insisted, "There is no hope at all. It is now a matter of hours!" Nevertheless, the commander still had hope and faith. He stood close beside the prostrate, unconscious form of his battered son in the hospital bed, and, following Jewish tradition, prayed in the darkened room, *Shema yisra'el adonai elohenu*— (i.e., Hear, O Israel, the Lord our God—). Abruptly, mysteriously, and miraculously, a weak and strained voice responded, *Adonai eḥad*! The Lord is one!"

Even in his delirium, these words in response emanated from the lips of the commander's son. Though otherwise unconscious, in some unfathomable manner, the boy had heard this prayer of hope from his father, a man unshakeable in his faith in the one God, who is the greatest physician of all. On hearing that prayer, the subconscious mind of the lad had somehow been inspired with the hope of revival. The commander told me that from that moment, his son's temperature had dropped, and he was miraculously restored to life. That boy lives today. The reason that he lives an almost normal life is because, when all seemed darkness and despair, both a father and a son together beheld the rainbow of God's eternal covenant.

VE-AHAVTA, OR "AND YOU SHALL LOVE"

The word *ve-ahavta* (i.e., "and you shall love") occurs three times in the Torah: First, you shall love your neighbor as yourself (Lev. 19:18); second, you shall love the stranger in your midst (Lev. 19:34); and finally, you shall love the Lord with all your heart (Deut. 6:5). A rabbi was asked why God is mentioned last. He answered, "If you do not love people, you cannot love God."

HASHKIVENU, OR "BE THERE"

The Kotsker Rebbe commented on the verse from Deuteronomy, "and God said to Moses, 'Go onto the mountain and be there.' "

Why was it necessary to have the words "be there"? God had already told him to go onto the mountain.

The rebbe answered that one can be on the mountain and not be there.

We can be in the synagogue at holiday services and not be there. We can be at home and not be there. Some talk to their wives, children, and parents, but they are not there.

The *Hashkivenu*, a prayer for peace, teaches us that we must be there. If we are to make peace, we must start with our families and our homes, our neighbors, and in business.

TIKU VA-ḤODESH SHOFAR, OR "SOUND THE *SHOFAR* ON THE NEW MOON"

In this prayer we read, *Ki ḥok le-yisra'el* (i.e., "It is a law for the children of Israel." God is saying to us, "The Jews must decide what the date of Rosh ha-Shanah is."

The rabbis tell us that the angels asked God, "When is Rosh ha-Shanah?" God replied, "Go to earth, and ask the Jewish people. It is up to man to set *Yom ha-Din*, the Day of Judgment!"

When we leave the synagogue this evening, we will notice in the sky the thin sliver of the moon. This signifies the new moon of Tishri. Hebrew months are determined by the phases of the moon. Therefore, today is not only Rosh ha-Shanah, but also *Rosh Ḥodesh*. For this reason, we recite the prayer *Tiku* ("Sound the *Shofar* at the New Moon").

TIKU VA-ḤODESH SHOFAR, OR "SOUND THE *SHOFAR* TO ANNOUNCE THE NEW MOON"

This prayer is recited because a new moon will be appearing in the sky this evening. The Jewish calendar is a lunar calendar (adjusted to the solar system) and that is why the new moon spells the beginning of Rosh ha-Shanah.

How can Tishri be the month of the New Year if the Bible tells us that Nisan is the month of the New Year? Nisan is the month of Passover, the liberation and freedom of the Jewish people and the beginning of the Jewish nation.

How did Tishri, the seventh month, become the first month on the religious calendar?

When the Temple was destroyed and our ancestors were exiled to Babylonia, they instituted the tradition of Tishri as the month of the New Year. Perhaps Ezra and Nehemiah were the first to introduce Tishri as the first month.

In the Talmud, Rabbi Eliezer stated, "The world was created in Tishri."

Rabbi Meir commented, "All the world is judged on Rosh ha-Shanah."

Undoubtedly, Tishri was the beginning of the New Year of the religious calendar, whereas Nisan was the first of the month of celebrating the founding of the Jewish people.

This is not a new phenomenon. In contemporary society, we have different days denoting the different new years (e.g., a fiscal year, a secular year, an income tax year, a sports season year, a fashion year, etc.).

Why does Rosh ha-Shanah come early on certain years and later in other years?

It has been aptly said that Rosh ha-Shanah never comes on time—it is always too early or too late!

In 1899, Rosh ha-Shanah occurred on September 5, and it will again be on September 5 in 2013.

The latest Rosh ha-Shanah celebrated in memory was October 4 in 1929 and once again in 1967.

Why does our religious calendar vary from year to year? How does one determine when the holidays occur or the date of a *Yahrzeit*?

The answer is in the prayer *Tiku*.

The new moon in the sky tonight will determine the new month of Tishri, which is the first of the month.

The Jewish calendar is a lunar calendar, twelve months of twenty-nine or thirty days, which causes us to lose eleven days a year. Therefore, we must adjust our lunar calendar to the solar calendar of 365 days. Just as a leap year is observed once in four years, which in actuality is a leap day on February 29, to adjust the loss of one day every four years on the secular calendar, so, too, an arrangement must be made to rectify the loss of eleven days a year when we adjust the lunar calendar to the solar calendar. For this adjustment, we add an entire month seven times in nineteen years, and designate it the second Adar, which is the twelfth month. This explains why Rosh ha-Shanah is early one year or later the next year. If there was no leap month during the previous year, then Rosh ha-Shanah arrives earlier. If there was a leap month, then Rosh ha-Shanah comes later.

This is an incredible calendar, which was instituted by Hillel II in the fourth century. Another amazing accomplishment is that our sages made certain that Yom Kippur would never occur on a Friday or a Sunday. If the Day of Atonement were to fall on a Friday, it would be impossible to return home and prepare a meal to break the fast, for the Sabbath would have begun. If it were to occur on a Sunday, it would be impossible for a family to prepare a final meal in the late afternoon of the Sabbath. Because of this, Rosh ha-Shanah will never fall on a Sunday and Monday or on a Wednesday and Thursday.

TEFILLAH BE-LAḤASH, OR "SILENT DEVOTION"

The story is told of a little boy whose parents died when he was three years old. Raised by a non-Jewish family, he knew nothing of his Jewish background.

Rummaging one day through his late mother's possessions he found an old prayerbook. He stared at it, realizing for the first time that he was of Jewish origin. He visited the little synagogue in his village on Yom Kippur. He listened to the strange language of Hebrew prayer.

He addressed God,

> God, I do not know how to pray or what to say. Here in my hand is my mother's prayerbook. May it pray the words to you on my behalf.

CHAPTER 3

ROSH HA-SHANAH

WHY DO WE COME?

Many are the reasons for attendance at High Holiday services: guilt, nostalgia, sentiment, family loyalty, conformity.

A powerful reason should be spirituality. Life is empty and material goods, luxuries, and conveniences do not make for fulfillment. We seek faith and hope, courage and inspiration.

We come because we want to identify with our people, be part or our historical tradition. We want to belong. There are probably as many different reasons for attendance as there are people in the synagogue on the High Holidays.

The real purpose of attendance is that we are in need of a spiritual check-up. Just as we bring our car to the automobile dealer every few months for a checkup, just as we visit our physician for an annual examination, so, too, we need a spiritual checkup. We need the inspiration of the High Holidays, the meaning and opportunity to lift ourselves up and dedicate ourselves once again to the values of our faith.

THREE-DAYS-A-YEAR JEWS

On the High Holidays, every rabbi feels the burden of a tremendous responsibility. Many of the congregants have not been in the synagogue since the last High Holidays. The rabbi has three days to share a message of the eternal values of Judaism, a message to inspire his congregation to strengthen their commitment to Jewish tradition in the months ahead.

The rabbi well knows of the "three days-a-year Jews," the "revolving-door Jews," and those who look upon the High Holidays as "instant Lent."

There is the "cardiac Jew," who is a Jew at heart, the "gastronomic Jew," who only likes Jewish food, and the "alimony Jew," who is willing to pay for it but has no relationship.

Then again, there is the "drop-in Jew," in for High Holidays or a Bar Mitzvah, the "drop-off Jew," who leaves her child off at Hebrew school, and the "drop-out Jew," who after Bar Mitzvah of his children leaves the synagogue.

It is not for the rabbi to castigate his people for not being more faithful in their attendance. Rather, the rabbi should be grateful that they are present at least for the High Holidays and that he is given the opportunity to inspire and lift them with a message, so that they will strengthen their commitment during the coming year to services, study, and observance.

There is a hasidic story describing customers who visit merchants for different reasons. Some come, examine all the merchandise, and do not make a purchase. They will return to services the following year.

Then there is the irritated customer who complains that it costs too much; the quality is not good; it is cheaper down the street. He does not buy a thing.

Then again, there is the customer who buys everything that he sees.

There is also the selective customer who purchases the most appealing merchandise.

What kind of customer are we for the High Holidays. Let us look at our portfolio of time, develop our priorities, and purchase wisely.

HONEY ON ROSH HA-SHANAH

Why honey? Why not candy, Sweet 'N Low (especially for the calorie-conscious), or some other sweetener.

One answer may be that although all of the above infuse sweetness, honey has an additional characteristic. It is sticky. Symbolically, we are expressing the hope that our noble resolutions and affirmations for the year ahead will not fade like a spiritual suntan but will stick with us throughout the year.

A second interpretation of the use of honey to express our wish for a sweet New Year is more realistic and practical. Yes, honey is indeed sweet, but it comes from bees and they often sting. The sweetness we are praying for can be accompanied by a sting, some form of pain and anguish that is an inevitable part of everyday life. Dipping apples or *hallah* in honey acknowledges that although we ask for sweetness, we must be prepared to deal with the irritations that are also part of everyone's life and human nature in general.

The bottom line is that eating apples or *hallah* dipped in honey is only a symbol. Every day in every way, each one of us must bring sweetness and kindness into the lives of every person to whom we relate. That will certainly make the prayer for a *shanah tovah u-metukah* not just a wish, but also a reality for the year.

A FRESH START

An angry reader once stormed into a newspaper office waving the day's paper, asking to see the editor of the obituary column. He showed him his name in the obituary listing. "'You see," he said, "I am very much alive. I demand a retraction!" The reporter replied, "I never retract a story. But I'll tell you what I'll do; I'll put you in the birth column and give you a fresh start!"

LE-EL OREKH DIN: THE DAY OF JUDGMENT

Eleazar Kallir comments that each line of the prayer begins with the letter *lamed*, which means "to," and then is followed by an alphabetical acrostic.

The first part of each line concludes with the word *din* (i.e., "judgment") and the second part concludes *be-yom din* (i.e., "on the Day of Judgment").

ADONAI ADONAI, OR "THE LORD, THE LORD"

A Kabbalistic interpretation of this prayer by the Ari, Rabbi Isaac Luria of Safed, relates that these words ensure us of God's mercy and give us the knowledge that God is always ready to forgive. These words were uttered at the conclusion of the biblical story of the Golden Calf, when Moses returned to Mount Sinai to receive the Ten Commandments a second time. These words mark the reconciliation of God and the Jewish people. Tradition has it that Moses returned to receive the Ten Commandments on the tenth of Tishri, the date of Yom Kippur.

KERI'AT HA-TORAH LE-YOM RISHON, OR "TORAH READING FOR THE FIRST DAY OF ROSH HA-SHANAH"

On the first day of Rosh ha-Shanah, we read of the birth of Isaac to Abraham and Sarah in their old age. We also read of Ishmael and his mother, Hagar, and the miracle of deliverance in the desert. We end with Abraham's covenant with Abimelech.

The connection with Rosh ha-Shanah is tied to the first words of the reading, "and the Lord remembered Sarah." Rosh ha-Shanah is a time of *Zikhronot* (i.e., remembering). The birth of Isaac reminds us that this marks the birth of the world and the birth of our character.

TORAH READING FOR THE FIRST DAY OF ROSH HA-SHANAH

We read of a dysfunctional family, Abraham, Sarah, and the other member of the triangle, Hagar. At Sarah's insistence, Abraham and Hagar give birth to Ishmael. The situation in Abraham's household was intolerable, for Isaac's birth precipitated the jealousy of Sarah and Hagar and the sibling rivalry of Isaac's brother Ishmael.

Sarah complains bitterly to Abraham. God admonishes Abraham, *shema bekolah* (i.e., "listen to her voice"). It is not Sarah's words that are important, but the sound of her voice. Abraham, from the sound of her voice, must hear how upset, anguished and frustrated his wife is. Abraham must discern the urgency, pain, hurt, heartbreak, pathos, alienation, and isolation in her voice. Sarah is a person, a human being. She is insecure, inadequate, and hostile. She suffers great pain and hurt.

In our relationships today, also, far more important than the words that are spoken, is the pain and anguish in the voice. Let us be sensitive to the pain of others.

HAFTARAH LE-YOM RISHON

The *haftarah* is from the Book of Samuel. Hannah, who is childless, vows that if she is blessed with a son, she will loan him to God. Eli, the High Priest, sees her lips moving and assumes that she is intoxicated. When she tells him of her vow, he assures her that she will be blessed with a son. Samuel is born, and the reading concludes with Hannah's prayer of gratitude to God, "I have loaned my son to the Lord." In the Torah reading, we read of the birth of Isaac, and in the *haftarah,* of the birth of Samuel. This is most appropriate for Rosh ha-Shanah, which signifies the birth of the world.

After the birth of Samuel, we read, "and Hannah brought her child to the Lord when he was young." The future of Judaism is in the hands of the mother. In our society, the father is usually away from home, at work, and the mother brings her child for religious education. It has been said aptly, "If you educate a boy, then you educate a father. But, if you educate a girl, you educate a family."

KERI'AT HA-TORAH LE-YOM SHENI, OR "TORAH READING FOR SECOND DAY OF ROSH HA-SHANAH"

Abraham was willing to offer his son as a sacrifice. We ask God to remember the merit of our ancestor. We sound the *shofar* to acknowledge the substitution of the ram that was caught in the thicket.

How could God demand of a father such an immoral act? Kierkegaard, in his book *Fear and Trembling,* develops the theory of the different levels of aesthetic, ethical, and absurd. Abraham's act fits the category of the absurd, he writes, because it requires a "leap of faith" to believe that God would demand something unethical of a father.

Kierkegaard failed to understand that the very first words, "and God tested Abraham," are the true meaning of the story. We, the omniscient reader, know that Abraham would not slay his son. Did Abraham have the faith to become the ancestor of the Jewish people? Was he prepared to sacrifice? This was God's test.

Religion and faith in God has no meaning unless we are willing to sacrifice.

AKEDAH, OR "THE BINDING OF ISAAC"

The paradox of this story is that Abraham, who is an advocate of righteousness, consents immediately to sacrifice his son. Abraham should have confronted God, the Lord of justice and mercy. Why was it necessary for God to test Abraham? God knew of Abraham's faith and commitment.

Why did Abraham consent to this immoral deed?

Why did Abraham not confront God as he argued with Him to spare the righteous people who lived in Sodom?

Why was there no resistance from Isaac?

These questions are not easily answered. Nevertheless, from the very first words of the story, we the omniscient readers are told that it was all a test.

AKEDAH: ANGELS ARE NEVER LATE

Rabbi Abraham Joshua Heschel writes that he cried the first time he heard the *Akedah* as a child. His father asked him why he was weeping, and he answered, "I was worried, papa. I was worried that the angel would be too late in calling to Abraham and telling him to stop."

"Don't worry, my son," his father said. "Angels are never too late. That is the way with angels, but people— people can be too late. That is the way with people."

People can be too late. This is true. We can be too late defending the downtrodden. We can be too late expressing gratitude, love, or concern. We can be too late reaching out to a member of our family or a neighbor or a friend. Angels are never late. However, people can be late.

AKEDAH: FATHER AND SON TOGETHER

Abraham and Isaac go forth to Mount Moriah, where Abraham is to sacrifice his only son as a test of his faith.

Twice the Bible says, "And Abraham and Isaac walked together." The rabbis comment, "One to slaughter and one to be slaughtered, one to kill and one to be killed. And yet they walked together, arm in arm and heart with heart."

The secret of Jewish survival is contained in this passage about the generations that have always walked together, parent and child.

For many, many centuries, this was the bastion of Jewish survival.

In recent times, with the tremendous influx of Jewish immigrants to the United States from the late 1880s, a separation soon developed between parent and child. The parents, who arrived with their Old World faith and foreign mannerisms, were not attracting the new generation to their way of life. Children rebelled. The child went one way and the parent went another.

Now in modern times, all too often, the generations are again "walking together." They are walking together the wrong way, to the wrong thing, away from Jewish values and Jewish traditions.

HAFTARAH LE-YOM SHENI

The *haftarah* from Jeremiah is the tender passage about Rachel. Jeremiah witnessed the destruction of the Temple and the Holy Land. He portrays Rachel, wife of Jacob, in her grave weeping bitterly, for she hears on the earth overhead the footsteps of her descendants going forth into exile. "Dry your eyes from tears, O Mother Rachel, for someday, your children will return."

After thousands of years of exile, the descendents of Mother Rachel have returned to the Holy Land. It is as if Mother Rachel, thousands of years later in her grave, hears overhead the footsteps of her descendants returning to *Erez Yisra'el*. This beautiful passage is read on Rosh ha-Shanah, which is a festival of hope and faith in the future.

SHOFAR

The *shofar* is an ancient Jewish symbol. It is a reminder of the sacrifice of Isaac, when the ram appeared in the thicket. In the time of Philo, Rosh ha-Shanah was also called *Ḥag ha-Shofrot* (i.e., the festival of the sounding of the *shofar*).

The *shofar* is an ancient musical instrument. It must be constructed from a kosher animal, usually a ram to associate it with the *Akedah* (i.e., sacrifice of Isaac). It may not be fashioned from a bull, for this would suggest the idolatry of the Golden Calf. In different countries and cultures, diverse animals are used: in North Africa, the ibex; in the Middle East, the African antelope or the gerenuk; in Yemen, the great kudu. These *shofrot* are long and twisted, emitting low tones. In Iraq, it is the evine; in Asia Minor, the hartebeest; in Australia, the merino sheep is used.

Oriental Jews prefer low solemn tones from the *shofar*. Ashkenazic Jews prefer higher notes of supplication.

No pictures are painted on the *shofar*. You do find decorations of carvings of biblical quotations.

In Jewish tradition, the *shofar* was sounded at the giving of the Ten Commandments, coronation of the king; advent of the Jubilee year; warning of natural disasters, for war, public announcements, national events, and so on, and upon the coming of the Messiah.

The earliest evidence of a *shofar* is on the capital of a first-century synagogue in Kefar Naḥum (i.e., Capernaum).

There are three distinct sounds of the *shofar*: *teki'ah* (i.e., a smooth, continuous note of joy and contentment), *teru'ah* (i.e., a minimum of nine "staccato" blasts depicting trepidation and sorrow), and *shevarim* (i.e., three short blasts).

It is traditional to sound the *shofar* a hundred times during the Rosh ha-Shanah service.

According to Maimonides, the purpose of Rosh ha-Shanah is to awaken those who slumber in spiritual lethargy. Saadiah Gaon was of the opinion that the *shofar* was sounded for all to acknowledge God in reverence. Eschatological theologians suggest that sounding the *shofar* will herald the Day of Judgment.

The prayer we recite to introduce the *shofar* is not *le-teko'ah shofar* (i.e., to sound the *shofar*), but rather *le-shemo'a* (i.e., to hear the sound of the *shofar*). We fulfill the *mitzvah* only when we hear the sounds of the *shofar* and take to heart the message that it proclaims.

SHOFAR

The *shofar* is not a mystical instrument whose sound will bring instant salvation. Originally, the *shofar* served as a trumpet or bugle. It sounded the call to march, war, danger, or peace. The sounding of the *shofar* is a call to action, the opportunity for self- scrutiny.

Originally, the *shofar* was sounded at the beginning of *tefillat shaḥarit* (i.e., early morning service). In Roman times, the townspeople might have misconstrued it as a signal for revolt. Therefore, the rabbis ordained that the *shofar* would be sounded later in the day at the *musaf* service.

SHOFAR

Saadiah Gaon finds not fewer than ten reasons for the sounding of the *shofar* on Rosh ha-Shanah.

The first reason is that this day is the beginning of creation. On it, God created the world, and he rules it. Just as it is with kings at the start of their reign—trumpets and horns are blown to make it known and heard in every place—thus it is when we designate the Creator as king on this day, as David said, "With trumpets and sound of *shofar*, shout ye before the king, the Lord" (Ps. 98:6)

The second reason is that the day of New Year is the first of the Ten Days of Penitence, so that the *shofar* is sounded on it as a warning, saying:

> Whoever wants to repent, let him repent; and if he does not, let him reproach himself. Thus do the kings. First they warn the people of their decrees, then if one violates a decree after the warning, his excuse is not accepted.

The third reason is to remind us of Mount Sinai, as it is said, "The sound of the *shofar* grew louder and louder" (Ex. 19:9).

The fourth reason is to remind us of the words of the prophets, which were compared to the sound of the *shofar* (Is. 58:1)

The fifth reason is to remind us of the destruction of the Temple and the sound of the battle cries of the enemies, as it is said, "Because thou hast heard, O my soul, the sound of the *shofar*, the alarm of war" (Jer. 4:19). When we hear the sound of the *shofar*, we will ask God to rebuild the Temple.

The sixth reason is to remind us of the binding of Isaac, who offered his life to heaven. We, too, declare our readiness to offer our lives for the sanctification of His name.

The seventh reason is so that when we hear the sound of the *shofar*, we will be fearful, we will tremble, and humble ourselves before the Creator, as it is written, "Shall the *shofar* be blown in a city and the people not tremble?" (Amos 3:6)

The eighth reason is to recall the day of the great judgment, as it is said, "The great day of the Lord is near . . . a day of the *shofar* and alarm" (Zeph. 1:14–16).

The ninth reason is to remind us of the ingathering of the scattered ones of Israel, which we ardently desire, as it is said, "And it shall come to pass in that day, that a great horn shall be blown, and they shall come that were lost in the land of Assyria . . . and they shall worship the Lord in the holy mountain at Jerusalem" (Is. 27:13).

The tenth reason is to remind us of the resurrection of the dead and the belief in it, as it is said, "All ye inhabitants of the world and ye dwellers on the earth, when an ensign is lifted up on the mountain, see ye, and when the *shofar* is blown, hear ye" (Is. 18:3).

SHOFAR

The holiday of Rosh ha-Shanah is called *Yom Teru'ah*, which means the "Day of the *Shofar* Blast."

The word *shofar* is derived from the Assyrian *sapparu*, meaning wild sheep of the ibex family.

Traditionally, the *shofar* is made from a ram's horn, although any horned animal may be used except a bull's horn because of its association with the Golden Calf.

Each *shofar* is unique and individual, since no two animals are alike.

The required curved shape of the *shofar* symbolizes the bent and humbled spirit beseeching God for forgiveness.

The *shofar* is the only musical instrument that has survived from ancient times to the present in its original form.

Traditionally, only the priests and Levites were allowed to blow the *shofar*, but in modern times, that restriction has changed.

The *shofar* is mentioned in the Bible seventy-two times. This is more than any other reference to a musical instrument.

The inside of the *shofar* may not be decorated, yet the outside surface may contain carved designs or gold overlay, but the mouthpiece must not be covered.

The *shofar* is not sounded on Shabbat. One reason is due to the possibility that the *ba'al teki'ah* may inadvertently carry the *shofar*, and carrying is forbidden on the Sabbath.

NO *SHOFAR* ON SHABBAT

When Rosh ha-Shanah occurs on the Sabbath, the *shofar* is not sounded. Obviously, the sanctity of the Sabbath surpasses even the sanctity of Rosh ha-Shanah.

However, there is a second message. That which is frequent takes priority to that which is infrequent. Some Jews return to the synagogue only for Rosh ha-Shanah and Yom Kippur. The Sabbath is observed every single week.

In life, too, we tend to emphasize that which is infrequent. The important days of our lives are birthdays, anniversaries, Mother's Day, Father's Day, and Thanksgiving.

However, we need weekly and daily reminders of the significance of these important days. Mother's Day is for every day. Father's Day is for every day. Thanksgiving should be for every day. We must seek God's presence every day and offer prayer every day.

Teshuvah is not just for Yom Kippur. Ethics and morality are for every day.

This is the reason that the Sabbath has priority to Rosh ha-Shanah, and that even the important ceremony of "Sounding the *Shofar*" on the New Year is eliminated if Rosh ha-Shanah occurs on the Sabbath.

SHOFAR

Anthropologists suggest that the sounding of a horn was normal in the liturgy of ancient man. The Jews did not invent the sounding of the *shofar*, but redirected the pagan meaning of sounding a loud noise on the New Year to frighten away demons.

This is an example of the genetic fallacy. What the ritual was in genetic origin has nothing to do with the meaning of its contemporary observance. The eating of pork is taboo in many societies. *Berit milah* in the ancient world might have been a puberty right. Breaking a glass at a wedding, in origin, might have been done to cast away the evil spirits. However, it is the reinterpretation and the spiritual meaning that impels us to observe these rituals today.

MIN HA-MEẒAR

The mystics in the prayer *Min ha-meẓar* read an acrostic *kara satan* (i.e., "Satan has been expelled").

THE NUMBER THREE

There are three blasts of the *shofar*. There are three strands of *tefillat musaf*: *Malkhuyyot*, *Zikhronot*, and *Shofarot*, and there are three sections with verses from the three sections of the Bible: the Torah, the Prophets, and the Writings.

THE SUMMONS OF THE *SHOFAR*

Ḥ. N. Bialik was very absent-minded. One day he boarded a train to Kiev to deliver an address on his poetic accomplishments. His wife bought the ticket for him, and she put it in his vest pocket. He dressed very quickly and forgot that the ticket was in his vest. The conductor approached and he realized that Bialik had no ticket.

The conductor said to him, "It's all right. I recognize you. You will pay for a new one now, and when you return home and find the ticket, it will be refunded to you."

Bialik replied, "Thank you very much, but that is not why I am concerned. I don't remember where I'm going."

We need direction, values, and priorities. This is the summons of the *shofar*.

HINENI HE-ANI MI-MA'AS: THE CANTOR'S PRAYER

Judaism is a down-to-earth religion. No one is perfect, not even a rabbi or cantor. Our religion endorses equality; everyone is on the same level. On the High Holidays, each of us must reach God directly through our own "channel." However, we do need the leadership and inspiration of the cantor. *Hīneni he-ani mi-ma'as* is the personal prayer of the humble cantor, aware of his own inadequacies, asking God to forgive him for his own personal sins because he is unworthy to represent the congregation.

Hīneni he-ani mi-ma'as was composed during the Middle Ages. It is a great burden that the cantor must bear in leading the service and inspiring the congregants to reach God. His prayer reveals his feelings of inadequacy in fulfilling this sacred task. *Hīneni he-ani mi-ma'as* expresses the fervor and devotion of the cantor, who is about to lead the *musaf*.

The story is told of Cantor Yosi of Slonim, who stood with the poor people at the entrance of synagogue at this point of the service. A choirboy would cry out, "Where is the cantor?"

The cantor would answer, *Hīneni* (i.e., "Here I am").

Another choirboy would exclaim, "Why is he standing at the entrance of the synagogue?"

He would answer, *he-Ani* (i.e., "I am poor").

A third choirboy would ask, "Is he asking for money?"

The cantor would reply, *mi-Ma'as* (i.e.,"I am poor in good deeds!").

The cantor would then walk slowly from the entrance of the synagogue to the *bimah* as chanting *Hīneni he-ani mi-ma'as*.

S. Y. Agnon tells the story of the *khapers*, who would kidnap young boys in Russia for lengthy service in the Russian army. Many of those who were kidnapped left Judaism. However, a handful sacrificed to remain Jewish.

He relates that Tsar Nicholas I once visited the synagogue in St. Petersburg on the Day of Atonement. The congregants asked who should be the cantor of *musaf*. They determined that rather than designate a scholar to lead the service, they would call upon a simple soldier who had served many years in the Russian army and retained his Jewish faith.

When we sacrifice to remain faithful, we merit the respect of the people.

KADDISH FOR *MUSAF*

The *Kaddish* is one of the most significant prayers in our liturgy. This prayer is recited before every silent devotion, at the end of a service, at the completion of a Torah reading, and also by those in mourning.

It is the sanctification of God. In the *Kaddish* recited by mourners, you might anticipate a mention of death or parents or immortality. Rather than this, the sanctification of God proclaims the lesson that life goes on; though we regard the past as precious. God is not mentioned in the *Kaddish* to teach that we hallow God's name through the redemption of life in this world.

There are different modes of the *Kaddish*: the *Ḥazi Kaddish* (i.e., the Half-*Kaddish*), the *Kaddish Shalem* (i.e., complete *Kaddish*), and the *Kaddish de-Rabbanan* (the Rabbis' *Kaddish*).

From the root word of *K-D-SH* we derive *Kiddush* (i.e., sanctification of the wine), *Kiddushin* (i.e., the marriage ceremony), and the *Kedushah* (i.e., holiness prayers after the silent devotion).

How did the *Kaddish* develop as a prayer for mourners? There is a theory that originally, the rabbinical *Kaddish* was recited by students after study of the Torah or Talmud. The occasion arose after the death of a teacher that, in his memory, his students would gather to recite the *Kaddish*.

"And my father was not a scholar!" people protested. Therefore, the tradition arose to recite the *Kaddish* for twelve months after a deceased parent.

The Talmud records that a wicked person required twelve months of recitation of the *Kaddish* for redemption from eternal punishment. To not classify a deceased parent in the category of a "wicked person," the tradition allows that the *Kaddish* be recited for eleven months and one day.

On the High Holidays, the word *le-ela u-le-ela* is added. God is exalted "even higher" on these holy days.

KADDISH FOR *MUSAF*

The familiar melody of the *musaf Kaddish* introduces the longest *Amidah* of the year. We shall interpret and explain as we proceed with this service. Please take your time in reciting your prayers. If you hum the *nusah* along with the cantor as he chants, he will take it as a compliment and an endorsement of his melody.

Prayer should not be perfunctory and recited by rote. *Kavvanah* or intent is most important. Prayer should be recited with sincerity. It is called *avodah she-ba-lev* (i.e., the service of the heart")—not only in the words of our prayers but also in the melody.

The story is told of an ignorant farmer who lost his way on the long journey to his synagogue on Rosh ha-Shanah. He found himself alone in the forest as the sun began to set. He had no *mahzor* with him. He addressed God and exclaimed, "I am an ignorant farmer and do not even have a prayer book on this evening of Rosh ha-Shanah. All I know are the letters, *alef, bet, gimmel, daled*. I shall recite these letters all evening and ask you to put them into words." God came to him in a dream that night and said, "All of your words have fallen into place. There was more sincerity in your prayers than those that emanated from your synagogue on Rosh ha-Shanah."

What is the most important word in the *mahzor*? I think everyone would agree that the word is *hayyim*. As we recite in every *Amidah, Zakhrenu le-hayyim* . . . (i.e., "Remember us for life, O King, who delights in life . . .").

However, we are asking for much more than life. We are praying, "O God, remember us in the year to come with many opportunities to say *Le-hayyim* over a cup of wine at a Bris, Bar or Bat Mitzvah, a child's wedding, the birth of a grandchild."

May it be Your will, O God, to let us shout *Le-hayyim* at a joyous family *simhah*. May this year truly be a year of joy, of Jewish family celebration and continuity as we lift our voices and cups in your praise.

Zakhrenu le-hayyim—remember us in the coming year and grant us *hayyim, simhot, nahat* for our families.

HAZARAT HA-SHELI'AH ZIBBUR, OR "THE REPETITION OF THE AMIDAH"

Some congregants feel that there is too much repetition in the High Holiday service; it is dull and uninspiring.

The repetition of the silent devotion is chanted by the cantor because repetition is part of the learning process; when we hear the cantor chant this service, it is an audiovisual method of learning; and this provided an opportunity for poets to compose *piyyutim* (i.e., commentaries that interpreted sections of the *Amidah*).

In the early centuries, prayers were not committed to writing. Many did not know the service by heart. Therefore, they appointed a *sheli'aḥ zibbur* (i.e., cantor) to chant it for them and enable them to follow.

U-NETANNEH TOKEF KEDUSHAT HA-YOM, OR "WE ACCLAIM THIS DAY'S PURE SANCTITY, ITS AWESOME POWER"

Legend has it that Rabbi Amnon of Mayence composed these words during the Middle Ages. There was a pogrom in his town and he was taken to the archbishop, who ruled that he must convert within three days. He refused and was tortured. His arms and legs were amputated. They brought him into the synagogue on the Day of Atonement, a dying husk of a man. In his last breath, he uttered this prayer, depicting unwavering faith in God.

This prayer denies fatal resignation that man's life is subject to irremediable fate. Man has within him the power to annul the severe decree. At the end of the prayer, we recite the three ways to avert the severe decree, with *teshuvah* (i.e., repentance), *zedakah* (i.e., good deeds), and *tefillah* (i.e., prayer). Repentance is something we do within ourselves. Charity and good deeds are between our neighbor and us. Prayer is the relationship of man to God.

The word "atonement" derives from three English words, at-one-ment. We attempt to achieve at-one-ment with God, with our fellow man, and with ourselves. The quantity of life may be in God's hands, but the quality of life is in man's hand.

The music of this prayer is unforgettable. It is the high point of the cantor's recitative. It evinces a wide range of motifs, from major to minor. First, we hear the majestic music of the heavenly court. Then comes the peal of the *shofar*. The angels tremble. Now, suddenly, we hear soothing pastoral melodies of a shepherd tending his flock. There follows a tearful supplication, "who will live, and who will die." Now the humble sigh, "Man is but dust." Finally, the prayer soars with the promise of "Thou Art God."

Teshuvah is not the desire to escape punishment, but rather to reestablish a relationship with God. The power of repentance is a most remarkable opportunity. We reappraise our deeds of the past and shape our behavior for the future.

The story is told of a pogrom in Eastern Europe. The entire village was destroyed. In the debris of ashes there sat a bearded Jew all alone in a booth.

"What are you doing?" a bystander asked.

"I am selling!"

"But we have no money."

"There is no need for money, I am selling faith."

Faith is the keynote of this prayer.

The great paradox of this prayer is that human destiny is in the hand of God. We recite, "who will live, and who will die?" However, man is not merely a puppet. Man can determine his own future. Man has free will.

Is it God who is inscribing our names in the book? Alternatively, is it man writing his own book?

We call this the *sefer ha-ḥayyim* (i.e., Book of Life). Will it be a live year or a dead year? "Who will live and who will die, who will be rich and who will be poor, who will be at peace and who will not be at peace. " On Rosh ha-Shanah, it is inscribed." Not God, but man is doing the writing. "Our character is determined not by what happens to us, but what we do in the face of circumstance."

Amazing, how a year can go by so quickly. We well remember last Rosh ha-Shanah as if it were yesterday, and the year before as if it were last week. An old man was asked, "What would you like for this coming year?" He replied, "Just one more *U-netanneh tokef*."

"Who will live and who will die" points to the uncertainty and the unpredictability of life. We never know, from month to month, from day to day, from hour to hour. "Man is like a breath, like a shadow that passes away." We never know from day to day—an accident, a heart attack, a stroke, an airplane crash. Who would believe that the seats next to us are empty this new year; sudden cancer, an unsuspected ailment, an accident in an automobile, a bus, or train.

Every day is precious, never to be repeated. Let us take advantage of every single hour. Let us take nothing for granted. Let us squeeze each opportunity dry, take advantage of every joy and pleasure. Let us embrace our loved ones and tell them that we care and what they mean to us.

We read in the Mishnah, "Act as though this day were your last." Obviously, we never know when our last day will come, so let us take full advantage of the opportunity as if this were our last day.

U-NETANNEH TOKEF

This prayer resembles a trial. It could be likened to a Roman military commander reviewing his troops. So, too, we all pass before God on the Day of Judgment.

Franz Kafka, in his memorable book *The Trial,* describes a helpless individual whom we only know by the letter K. We do not know what his crime is. We are not told who the accused or the judges are. The entire novel relates to his search for an answer to these questions.

We who are here today do not confront a cruel and unknown judge. We recall our deeds of the past year and acknowledge that we are responsible.

These ten days comprise an unusual trial. Most trials determine responsibility for past deeds. This trial determines what we will do about our future actions.

The legend has it that Rabbi Amnon of Mayence composed this prayer in the eleventh century in the synagogue as he died a martyr for his commitment and rejected apostasy. It is an unforgettable story, but the purpose of Rosh ha-Shanah is not martyrdom, but rather human responsibility and the possibility of changing our characters.

There is terrible violence among our young people. We read of senseless shootings in public schools. Children eleven- and twelve-years-old are shooting their teachers and classmates.

What is their motivation? Many answer, "We are bored." What does it mean to be bored? It means that the child wants something to do, some excitement, recognition and acceptance. This is the moral bankruptcy of our society.

As children, were we ever bored? We always were content to play baseball, read a book, go to a movie, even practice the piano, and do homework.

If children are bored, must they take a gun and hurt someone, shed blood?

U-netanneh tokef should inspire us to return to our ethical and moral values, that human life is sacred, that we have a mission for *Tikkun Olam* (i.e., Repair of the World).

U-NETANNEH TOKEF

U-netanneh tokef reminds us how swiftly this past year has gone by. We cannot believe that it is an entire year since we gathered for Rosh ha-Shanah. It is like yesterday, two years ago, like the week before. Perhaps on Rosh ha-Shanah we should ask God "to slow life down." We must cherish and squeeze every moment dry.

On the other hand, when life goes by quickly, it attests to the fact that we are happy.

Would the alternative be to "slow life down" and be unhappy? Some people count the hours and count the days.

Every day is a blessing from God.

We take a breath eighteen times a minute, 1,080 times an hour, and 25,920 times a day. We barely notice the fact that we are taking breaths. By the age of forty, we will have taken 378 million breaths. Each breath is a measured gift from the hand of God.

Do you think this is an exaggeration? Ask the asthmatic. or the one afflicted with cystic fibrosis or emphysema. We take 25,000 breaths a day; we should thank God 25,000 times a day for this great gift in sustaining our life.

On Rosh ha-Shanah, we are aware of the uncertainty of life. How unpredictable life really is! You never know from day-to-day; an airplane crash, an automobile accident, a heart attack. This prayer admonishes us that every moment is precious; that we should cherish and take advantage of every opportunity that comes our way. William Lyon Phelps addressed his opening class in English literature at Yale University, "Gentlemen, I have the secret of happiness. Pretend, when you rise from bed in the morning, that this is the first day of your life; you are overwhelmed with the awe and wonder of all that you see for the first time. Your heart is filled with gratitude." On the other hand, "pretend," he said, "that this is the last day of your life, never to be repeated, never to experience it again."

The story is told of a wise man, who was approached by a disciple.

"I ask you, learned sage, is the bird in my hand dead or alive?"

This was a trap. If the wise man said that the bird was dead, then he would open his hand and the bird would fly away. If he said that the bird was alive, then he would crush the bird in his hands and show the sage that he was wrong. Answered the wise man, "It is all in the power of your hands!"

The quantity of our lives is not in our hands. However, the quality of our lives is up to us.

For the duration of *U-netanneh tokef*, we think of two things. We are filled with hope. No matter the events of the past year, we are offered a fresh start, a new challenge, a new opportunity, a new leaf. We thank God that this year is ended. We thought it would never end with its problems and *zarot* and *shever lev*. We have all experienced problems this past year: illness, bereavement, reverses, family tensions, business reverses, disappointment, and loneliness. We say to each other, "May next year be better." However, we hastily add, "At the very least, may it be no worse!"

The second reaction is sadness. The year has gone by so swiftly. Last Rosh ha-Shanah seems to have occurred just last week. We say to ourselves, "A whole year has gone by and we have hardly had time to relax and catch our breath." "Man is like unto a breath, his days are as a shadow that passes away." We experience sadness that the year has slipped by so quickly, that time has gone so fast. Before we know it, life is ended. "We are like the grass that withers, the flower that fades, a fleeting shadow, a passing cloud, like the dust that vanishes."

A man once took his old car to a dealer and asked him to sell it for him. When the dealer asked how many miles were on it, the man replied, "It's got 230,000 miles." The salesperson replied, "This is illegal advice, my friend, but it will never sell unless you turn back the mileage." The man left.

When the car salesperson had not heard from the man for several weeks, he called him. "I thought you were going to sell that old car."

"I don't have to anymore!" he answered brightly. "It's only got 77,000 miles on it now. Why should I sell it?"

The story illustrates a spiritual truth. Too many people today are only fooling themselves if they think that they are pleasing God just by changing their external behavior. What is needed is real *teshuvah*, genuine change of path.

The old car still had a sick engine, bad rings, and a transmission that slipped. Turning back the odometer does not change any of that. Similarly, just coming to synagogue on Rosh ha-Shanah and Yom Kippur, mouthing the prayers, and standing and sitting on command will not purge us of sin. Only repentance, prayer, and charity will avert the severe decree.

The *U-netanneh tokef* tells us to take an account of the past and attempt to purge ourselves of foolishness and pettiness.

The great Hebrew and Yiddish author I. L. Peretz tells the story of Bonche Schweig. Poverty stricken, persecuted, harassed, and exploited in life, he always bore his burdens in silence. He never complained and never murmured.

When he died, he was offered in heaven a reward for bearing his burden so stoically. "You will be granted one wish, what do you ask for?"

"I think I will have a fresh hot bagel with butter."

This seems to be an example of the foolishness, the pettiness, and the trivia that are so important to us in life.

On a higher plane, this story was a strong protest against the devastating effect of poverty on the human soul. Bonche Schweig was the typical dumb sufferer, bearing injustice and insult in silence. On earth, he made no impression, but in heaven, he caused a great stir. The highlight of his life was a hot bagel. During his lifetime, he was often hungry and often denied a dry crust of bread. Because of devastating poverty, all he could wish for was a hot bagel. Bonche never indulged in tirades against social injustice, but his answer in this story speaks volumes.

MI YIHYEH, OR "WHO WILL LIVE AND WHO WILL DIE"

"Who by fire and who by earthquake."

After the 1994 earthquake in Los Angeles, a local rabbi, Edward Feinstein of Valley Beth Shalom, described his conversation with a representative from the Allstate Insurance Company. The agent looked at the list of items that were damaged and asked "Why six sets of dishes?"

The rabbi answered, "One is for the Sabbath, one for Passover, one for weekday, and for each set there is *fleishig* (i.e., meat) and *milchig* (i.e., milk).

"Would you please spell *fleishig* for me," the agent asked.

After the rabbi carefully explained the laws of *kashrut* and the separation of milk and meat, the insurance agent said, "Why do you do this?"

Replied the rabbi, "Because by this observance, I come closer to God."

Asked the agent, "If you come close to God, why would He allow an earthquake to destroy your property?"

The rabbi replied, "So that He might bring me an Allstate representative."

TESHUVAH, OR "REPENTANCE"

The *U-netanneh tokef* concludes that there are three ways to avert the severe decree, by *teshuvah*, (i.e., repentance), by *tefillah* (i.e., prayer), and by *zedakah* (i.e., charity).

Repentance entails one's relationship to himself. Prayer has to do with one's relationship to God. Charity has to do with relationships to others. It is a concrete manifestation of inner peace and spiritual strength.

The *vav* (i.e., the conjunction "and") separating the three ways to avert the evil decree is a coordinating conjunction. These are not three independent items, each capable of averting the severe decree. These three actions are interrelated and concern the depth of our repentance, the quality of our prayer and will ultimately be measured by our charity and good deeds.

KOL MA-AMINIM, OR "ALL WHO BELIEVE"

Not too long ago, on a graffiti wall at St. John's University, these words were written: "God said unto them, 'Who do you say that I am?' They replied, 'You are the eschatological manifestation of the ground of our being. You are the charisma in which we find the ultimate meaning of our interpersonal relationships.' God said. 'What?' "

All definitions of God are doomed to failure because the finite mind cannot define the infinite. We cannot see God and cannot feel God, but we can learn the will of God through the moral and ethical demands of His Torah.

"When we touch our fellow human being, we touch God, because God is within each of us." Love your fellow human beings and you love God. Serve your fellow human beings and you serve God.

In fact, when we read the *mahzor*, we find little about God's nature. The focus is on our nature. The liturgy is not an exercise in "speculative theology," an attempt to consider God's qualities and God's acts. The liturgy is essentially a practical guide, focusing on human activity and on ethics, not on what God does, but on what we do, not on God's powers but on our weaknesses and strengths. Rosh ha-Shanah is not devoted to the passive appreciation of God's wonders in nature, but to an active consideration of our purpose and our responsibilities.

To sit in the synagogue on Rosh ha-Shanah is not to think about God, but to think about ourselves in relation to God, not to see ourselves as sinners, but as potential sanctifiers, and thus to connect the idea of goodness with Godliness.

From Rosh ha-Shanah, we learn that although God is the creator of the world, we are the molders of history and society. God created the world, but we help determine its destiny. Our prayers remind us of the wonderful potential we have to raise the level of our living and to give significant meaning to what we do.

As the psalmist put it, "The heavens are the heavens of the Lord, but the earth is given to Man." May we act nobly and righteously. May we be worthy.

Every individual has his faith. Whether we recognize it or not, whether we avow it or not, the beliefs that we really hold are not necessarily those we affirm with our mouth, but those that are operative in our life. The real decision is thus not between faith and no-faith, but between faith in some false absolute, in some synthetic idol—the construction of our hands or heart or mind—or faith in the true Absolute, the transcendent God. This is a decision that wrenches our whole being. For it means a decision for the last time to abandon all efforts to find the center of existence within one's own self, but rather a decision to commit oneself to God without qualification or reservation.

ALEINU LE-SHABBE'AḤ, OR "IT IS FOR US TO PRAY"

It would be impossible to explain fully the riddle of Jewish history and the endurance of the Jew without taking into account the power, the strength, and the stamina that belief in himself as one of the Chosen People affords him. Nor can there be an intellectually satisfying rationale for continued Jewish survival unless, at the core of our religious convictions, there is retained the awareness of an indissoluble covenant between God and Israel—not merely a vague feeling of communal solidarity, but a sense of collective commitment and historic purpose.

MALKHUYYOT, ZIKHRONOT, SHOFAROT

Literally, these three strands of the musaf depict God the King, God Remembers, and God Reveals. Allegorically, these poetic symbols contain profound insight.

When we call God a King, we refer to the sovereignty of God in the Universe. We have faith that there is purpose and meaning, direction and order in life and in the world.

When we say that God remembers, we assert that there is memory in human experience. Good is remembered and evil is remembered. We Jews have long memories; we remember both our friends and our enemies. We also remember that at times in life, it is better not to remember.

God the Revealer implies divine inspiration. God reveals his genius to Moses and the Prophets, to sages and scholars in every generation. God is the inspiration for musicians and artists, poets and scientists. In addition, we reveal ourselves to others and others reveal themselves to us.

MALKHUYYOT: GOD, THE SOURCE OF VALUES

The *maggid* of Dubno tells the story of an archer who shot arrows at a wall. Afterward, the people painted targets around each hole, so that each shot became a bull's eye.

Oftentimes, we value an object because we pursue it. We do not pursue an object because we value it.

ZIKHRONOT, OR "REMEMBRANCES"

On Rosh ha-Shanah, we want God to remember our good deeds of the past year. On the other hand, life would be intolerable if we could not on occasion forget.

Oftentimes, we remember too much—a slight, an insult, ingratitude, a harsh word. Sometimes, we must remember what to forget. Let us remember that someday we will be forgotten.

ZOKHER KOL HA-NISHKAḤOT, OR "REMEMBERING THE FORGOTTEN"

Our rabbis tell us, "If you perform a good deed and boast about it, then God forgets it." On the other hand, "if you perform a good deed and forget about it, then God remembers it."

The rabbis continue, "If you commit a sin and forget about it, then God remembers it. If you commit a sin and remember it, then God forgets it."

Rabbi Moshe Lieb, the Sasover Rebbe, concludes, "God remembers only what man forgets."

MODIM ANAḤNU LAKH

"We thank you . . . for Your miracles, which are daily with us, and for Your wondrous kindness at all times."

We all have our share of problems; life is never completely smooth. Ill health, reverses, family dilemmas . . . we all carry our burdens. Nevertheless, would we trade our tensions and anxieties with those of others? At least we know what troubles us; our neighbor's lot may be even worse. We somehow manage to muddle through and cope as best we can. Could we really handle someone else's misfortunes?

Members of a synagogue were constantly complaining to their rabbi of their misfortunes and disgruntlements. He gathered them together and distributed paper sacks to everyone assembled.

"On slips of paper, write each of your problems and complaints, place them in your sack, and deposit them on the pulpit." They complied.

"And now," he instructed, "take any sack you want. Trade in your problems for someone else's bag."

Do you know what happened? Everyone took back his own sack. Better our own problems than someone else's.

There is so much misery and unhappiness in our midst—poverty, hunger, malignancy, affliction, mental illness, retardation, divorce, broken homes, animosity, loneliness—thank God for what we don't have.

You remember the observation, "I was unhappy because I had no shoes until I saw a man who had no feet."

We always complain, "Why did this have to happen to me?" We face surgery, lose our job, a fire destroys our home, the family car is wrecked in an accident. "Why did this have to happen to me?" Why do not we respond the same way when we are blessed with good fortune? We move into a new home, our daughter graduates from college, we receive a promotion, the stock market rises—"Why did this have to happen to me?"

A poor man had a problem and sought the advice of his rabbi. "I'm so poor. I live in a two-room hut with my wife and five children. It is so crowded, so noisy, so hot, so unbearable. I can't stand it any longer."

Replied the sage, "Bring a goat and two chickens into your house, and then return next week."

When the week was up, the poor, harassed man returned to the rabbi.

"It's impossible. My children, the chickens, the goat, all together. The bedlam, the odors, the stench, the bleating, and cackling. I'm going out of my mind!"

"Remove the chickens and the goat!" advised the rabbi.

The next day the poor man returned.

"Rabbi, thank you, thank you. I love my little home. It is so quiet, so calm, and peaceful. Thank you for your wonderful advice."

SIM SHALOM

In this prayer, we ask God to remember us in his book of life, blessing, peace, and *parnasah tovah* (i.e., "good security").

This is a rather peculiar request, for we are qualifying security with the adjective "good." *Parnasah* means financial security, a job, and sufficient sustenance with which to provide a family. However, what makes *parnasah* "good"?

A decent living means enough to sustain a family and enjoy some of the pleasures and luxuries of life.

Parnasah tovah means to earn money in a "good" way with honesty, integrity, responsibility, and concern for employees and associates.

To earn money in a "good" way refers to what the money does to us. If our livelihood causes us tension and anxiety, agitation, and time away from spouse and family, then it is not the kind of livelihood the rabbis envisioned.

Good *parnasah* refers to doing *tovah*, sharing our wealth and performing good deeds.

SIM SHALOM

On the High Holidays, we ask God for his choicest gifts: life, blessing, peace, and prosperity. However, we ask this not only for ourselves as individuals, but also for the entire Jewish people. "For us and for all your People, the House of Israel."

CHAPTER 4
KOL NIDREI

YOM KIPPUR

The Day of Atonement conditions us to suspend ourselves from the world. It is almost parallel to death. We do not eat, but fast. We wear a white *kitel*, which is symbolic of shrouds. The *tallit*, which we wear on *Kol Nidrei* night, symbolizes the *tallit* we take to our grave. Prohibitions against washing, bathing, sexual relationships, and the use of leather all suggest withdrawal from the world.

In Jerusalem, the southern gate to the Old City, the one closest to the *Kotel*, is known as the Dung Gate, *Sha'ar ha-Ashpot*, the Gate of Filth. The usual explanation is that when the old City was in Turkish or Arab hands, garbage would be dumped there to make it harder for Jews who wanted to go to the *Kotel*. However, among the legends of Old Jerusalem is another explanation. It teaches that Jewish pilgrims would come to Jerusalem from all throughout the world to pray at the wall. They would come on foot across the desert. By the time they reached the gates of the city, their feet would be covered by mud and dirt. They did not want to defile the Temple Mount by entering the city in that condition, so they would wash all the mud and filth off their feet at that southern gate.

We stand tonight at the gate leading to a New Year. We want to enter it clean and undefiled. We ask Yom Kippur to cleanse us of all those old habits and resentment—the need always to be right, the feeling that we have to be perfect, the fear that no one will love us if they find out we did something wrong, the anger we feel at parents and children, husbands and wives, who have problems that we can't solve, whom we resent for making us feel incompetent because we can't solve their problems when all they really want from us is our love and acceptance, not some magic wand. Throughout the past year, we have been burdened by those feelings and that is why the year was not as good as it might have been.

Only if we wash ourselves clean of those resentments, those expectations, those fears, only then can we walk through the gate and claim the good New Year that awaits us.

Unique among evening services, on *Kol Nidrei*, a *tallit* is worn. One explanation is that at the time of judgment, this extra element of protection helps us to feel safe.

Rabbi David Wolpe comments that coverings are very important in the Jewish tradition. Not only a *tallit*, but a *kippah* is a covering as well. So are structures under which Jewish life is built—the synagogue, the *sukkah*, and the *ḥuppah*. In the evening prayer *Hashkivenu*, we ask God to spread a covering of peace over us.

The world is an often hostile place. We built all sorts of bulwarks against the elements, emotional and physical. We fashion homes and seek refuge in families and communities. The portrait of an anguished individual—Lear raging, Ahab struggling with a tossing ship—is often an image of those with no covering, exposed to the furies of elemental forces. In a mystical bedtime prayer, we pray that angels might stand not just on each side of us, but also above us, covering us, sheltering us. We pray for the *Shekhinah*, the presence of God.

Yom Kippur is a time we stand revealed, and even afraid. We pray that God spreads a covering of health, happiness, and peace over all of us. May the coming year find us sheltered and warm.

TESHUVAH, OR "REPENTANCE"

On Erev Yom Kippur, a ḥasidic rebbe sat with his three disciples, trying to prepare them for the lessons of *teshuvah*, of repentance. To each disciple, he asked, "What were your sins this year?"

"Rebbe," the first disciple replied, "I know that I sinned one terrible sin this year."

"Go then," the rebbe said to him, "and find me one large stone."

The second disciple said, "Rebbe, I sinned a few times this year."

"Go then," the rebbe answered, "and find me four or five stones."

The third disciple approached. "I sinned many small times, little, different, even inconsequential things. I can't remember each and every one."

"Go then," the rebbe said to him, "and find me many small stones."

The disciples left and went about their tasks. When they returned, the rebbe spoke to them.

"Now go back to the street," he instructed, "and replace the stones you have brought to exactly the same spot from where you took each and every one."

The disciples ran out and preformed this task. All but the third returned. He was gone all day. Just moments before the *shofar* was to be sounded, he ran into the *shul*.

"Rebbe," he cried, "I searched and searched all night and all day to find each exact spot of my small stones. I simply could not do it."

"So it is with sins," the rebbe taught. "The large are easy to remember, and thus to rectify. However, you can never remember all the little and seemingly inconsequential ones; and the task of correcting every one is so arduous, it could take a lifetime, and you might never be able to fulfill that. That is why you must correct each as it happens, or you will be left with the little things to burden your life and weigh down your heart."

PLAYOFFS OR WORLD SERIES

When Yom Kippur occurs, there is always competition from baseball. Now that the baseball season has been extended, it is rare that the World Series takes place on Yom Kippur. I remember as a child when everyone would be telling the score of the World Series. The rabbi even announced the World Series score before *Aleinu le-shabbe'aḥ*.

A rabbi was once impressed by a congregant who was wrapped in his *tallit* the entire day. Little did he know that a transistor radio was hidden there so that the man could keep abreast of the World Series.

How interesting that during the World Series we all become *mevinim*, experts. During the year, many could not care less about baseball.

The concept of "playoff" is intriguing. In a way, the High Holidays are our personal "playoffs." "Did we do our best on the field?" "Are we behind or ahead?" "Were there heartbreaks or thrills?" "Are we losers or winners?" The season is done and the World Series will begin. A pundit once termed Yom Kippur as "World Serious."

However, in this playoff, who was our real opponent? God? Our neighbor? Our opponent, primarily ourselves, our weaknesses and flaws, our temptations and *Yezer ha-Ra'*. To be victorious we must spend time training, conditioning ourselves, practicing constantly, and achieving control of our minds and bodies.

KOL NIDREI, OR "ALL VOWS"

The cantor recites the first version very quietly as if we are approaching the King with fear. In the second recitation, he raises his voice a bit more, as if taking a chance. The third recitation of *Kol Nidrei* is much louder, for the cantor now feels at home.

Another explanation is that the first recitation is one of contrition and a plea for forgiveness. The second *Kol Nidrei* is based on hope for the mercy of God. The third recitation expresses the confidence that God will forgive us and inscribe us for life.

Kol Nidrei puts us in a spiritual mood so that we willingly leave behind the essentials of life, food, drink, possessions, sexual activity, and care of our body. We attempt on Yom Kippur to find that which is truly important to us in life. We look to the source of life and affirm that it does not rest in the world, but resides in God, whom we cannot fathom. *Kol Nidrei* urges us to strip away our pretensions that "we are righteous and have not sinned." However, we have sinned.

We wrap ourselves in symbols of eternity and direct ourselves to the symbol of authority. We refuse all that would defile us and separate us from the Divine. The spirit of renewal just begins with the *Kol Nidrei*. It is only the first act of a five act drama that leads to *shaḥarit, musaf, minḥah,* and *Ne'ilah*. Only if we take the entire drama, all five acts, seriously, will we attain a complete transformation.

The *Kol Nidrei* is an ancient, legal formula in which we attempt to absolve ourselves of rash promises. The setting on the pulpit is a *bet din*, a court of law. For that reason, the formula is recited three times. Since a court of law must assemble before dark, it is the only holiday that does not begin with absolute sunset. Therefore, we place the *tallit* around our shoulders because it is still light.

Judaism demands respect for the vows, promises, and obligations we take upon ourselves. It is a prayer that extols integrity—that we mean what we say and say what we mean.

The Bible tells us, "If you make a vow, do not delay to fulfill it." We read in the Book of Ecclesiastes, "It is better not to make a vow than to promise and not fulfill."

Society could not possibly exist unless we take seriously and honor our vows and obligations. There could be no marriage, business, government, or community without honoring our promises and obligations. We say of a person, "his word is his bond." Therefore, we start Yom Kippur releasing ourselves from the guilt of unfulfilled vows, so that next year we may realize that they must be sanctified.

Kol Nidrei is recited three times, a mystical number, corresponding to the three forefathers, Abraham, Isaac, and Jacob. In addition, three are necessary for a *mezuman*.

Kol Nidrei is a very mysterious and eerie introduction to Yom Kippur. Even more than the words, which are in reality a dry, legal formula in Aramaic, it is the music that touches the heart. All of the Scrolls of the Torah have been removed from the Ark, worshippers are wrapped in the *tallit*, and families are all sitting together. The color white is predominant; the white Torah covers, the *kitel* (i.e., gown), women's clothing is white, the symbol of purity. The music is haunting in a minor key; someone described the *Kol Nidrei* as "a formula wrapped in a melody." *Kol Nidrei* is the soul of the Jew, encompassing the history of our people—the pathos and jubilation, the triumph and tragedy, the tears and laughter, the pride, glory, and dignity.

Franz Rosenzweig describes in his diary an unforgettable episode that occurred in his youth. He was flirting with conversion to Christianity, and so informed his mother. On *Kol Nidrei* night, he was wandering the streets of Berlin and heard sounds of music emanating from a building. He entered; it was a *Kol Nidrei* service and he viewed all of the scrolls of the Torah removed from the ark and all of the men wrapped in the *tallit* in prayer. He remained for the entire service and then the next day. He was so moved and mesmerized by the service that he determined to retain his Jewish identify. He began to study Torah as a serious student and became one of the great Jewish thinkers of the last century.

For the Marranos of Spain, *Kol Nidrei* must have provided a most meaningful catharsis. To save their lives, they pretended to practice Christianity outwardly, but remained Jews inwardly. Only once a year, on *Kol Nidrei*, were they able to gather in secret as Jews and worship according to their tradition. When they began *Kol Nidrei* with the words "absolve us from rash promises made this past year," it struck a resonant chord in their hearts for forgiveness for forced vows to Christianity.

We ask forgiveness from God, from our neighbor, and resolve to grant forgiveness to others who have wronged us. It was the custom on the afternoon before *Kol Nidrei* to visit the homes and the shops, seek forgiveness, and ask for forgiveness.

Some of us can never bring ourselves around to forgiving. How can we ask God to forgive us if we are not prepared to forgive others? Rabbi Meir once refused to begin the *Kol Nidrei* service in his synagogue until everyone had turned to his neighbor and asked for forgiveness. What if we halted our own service and appealed to our people to do the same?

The story is told of a man who approached his rabbi and said, "I made confession on Yom Kippur and I still feel miserable."

The rabbi answered, "You have confessed to God, and he has forgiven you. Now go out and ask forgiveness from your neighbor."

Having done this, the man returned to the rabbi and said, "I still feel miserable."

The rabbi replied, "Now forgive yourself!"

Some of us are haunted by guilt even if we have forgiven and been forgiven. The New Year provides us the opportunity to forgive others and yet reminds us that we are human and make mistakes. We must also learn to forgive ourselves.

KOL NIDREI: NEUTRALIZING OATHS BOTH PAST AND FUTURE

All vows, oaths, and promises that we made to God from last Yom Kippur and were not able to fulfill—may all such vows between God and us be annulled. May they be void and of no effect. May we all be absolved of and released from them.

The *Kol Nidrei* prayer, chanted in the synagogue at the beginning of the Yom Kippur Eve service, was introduced into the liturgy with the approval of a variety of sages. The prayer was later challenged by halakhists, and in the nineteenth century, by Reform rabbis who even omitted it from the prayerbook in Western European communities. Furthermore, antagonists of the Jewish people frequently cited the prayer in their assertions that a Jew's oath may be annulled and is not to be believed. Hence, many lawmakers saw fit to create a special "Jewish oath," but other judges denied the Jews' use of this oath, citing *Kol Nidrei*.

In Paris, in 1240, Rabbi Yeḥiel came forward to defend *Kol Nidrei*. He emphasized to his fellow Jews that the prayer referred only to internal vows, not related to anyone outside of the Jewish community.

Rabbi Yeruḥam ben Meshullam, who lived in Provence in the twelfth century, challenged the "stupid" people who made vows light-heartedly, assuming that *Kol Nidrei* would nullify them. He ruled that such individuals were not qualified to take an oath.

The *Kol Nidrei* prayer has been a center of controversy for many centuries. Some suggest that *Kol Nidrei* only refers to vows made voluntarily; others, to the contrary, consider that the prayer refers to vows given under duress. In actuality, it appears that the author of the text of *Kol Nidrei* surely meant something simple, clear, and reasonable. That is why it is wrong to assume that *Kol Nidrei* calls on people to give up all their obligations or some part of them.

The custom of vowing or swearing by God's name predates the Third Commandment and may be as old as human speech. People swore by what was most precious to them—by valuable objects, by their own life, by parts of their body, by freedom, by their relatives as well as by various divine images. In the monotheistic faiths, this pattern of speech quickly grew into abusive swearing. It is unknown when and where *Kol Nidrei* came into being. Nevertheless, there are grounds for assuming its intention was to neutralize formulas or oaths connected with God's name. The goal of the purist in this struggle was to disavow oaths, that is, to proclaim them sacrilegious and devoid of any meaning or authority.

Furthermore, if people cannot help uttering God's name in vain and swearing by His name, *Kol Nidrei*, along with the Third Commandment, declared in advance all swearing is void of any significance. An individual uttering *Kol Nidrei* three times on Yom Kippur repents in advance for all possible swearing, any oaths that by accident, or for any other reason, he may link with God's name. "May they be considered obliterated . . . invalid and of no force. They will not bind us and have no power of us . . ."

The plural in this formula—"us," "above us"—implies not only those who transgress the commandment, but also each pair of partners to an oath, the one making it and the one accepting it. The oath lies in the word itself. The word ought to be truthful. Truth and strength are in the word itself and not in the accompanying phrases of authority. To limit the number of such phrases or omit them all together, especially those that transgress the Third Commandment, *Kol Nidrei* declared them void a priori, before they were even uttered.

This concept espoused by the author of *Kol Nidrei* was obvious to his contemporaries. In the course of time, due to the brevity of the prayer, its original meaning has become less clear and ultimately has been completely forgotten.

The current essence of *Kol Nidrei* is based on the supposition that the initial meaning of the prayer in the course of time was forgotten. All that was left of the original creation of the unknown ancient author was the shell.

A similar phenomenon is known in ethnography, which often can explain the sense of folk customs, legends, and so on. Sometimes, it is possible to reconstruct the etymological motivations of words and ethnological motivations of customs. If the present analysis of *Kol Nidrei* is valid, it belongs in the realm of such reconstructions.

This analysis of the original sense of *Kol Nidrei* may be compared to the Christian custom of "swearing on the Bible" or "kissing the Cross." In the Christian world, it was considered that only oaths of this nature could have binding force whereas any Jewish oath, taking into account the exterior meaning of

Kol Nidrei, had no such power. However, as the courtroom practice shows, swearing on the Bible and kissing the Cross have meaning only for people who tell the truth without any oath.

It should be assumed that the author of *Kol Nidrei* had something like this in mind. He was telling the people, as it were, "We should not swear by the name of the Almighty. All the oaths are in vain. Let every word of ours be true—then the oaths will disappear by themselves."

The Torah demands respect for vows: "When you make a vow to the Lord your God, you shall not delay in fulfilling it, for then you will have sinned, as the Lord requires fulfillment of all vows. Nevertheless, you do not sin if you refrain from vowing. You must be careful to fulfill any vow to the Lord which has passed your lips" (Deut. 23:22–24). Moreover, Ecclesiastes states, "Be not rash with your mouth, nor let your heart be hasty to utter a word before God.

In spite of such instruction and our own experience, we do make rash or foolish vows that cannot or should not be fulfilled. Jewish tradition did not want to relieve an individual of the obligation to fulfill his vows; yet it did want to allow a person to annul a vow the fulfillment of which could cause harm. At the start of Yom Kippur in particular, tradition also wanted to relieve the individual of guilt he might feel for an unfulfilled vow, even a harmless one. It therefore devised a comprehensive legal formula of dispensation solemnly and publicly retracting all vows. The rabbis teach, "Whoever wishes all the vows he may make throughout the year to be null and void shall say at the beginning of the year, 'May all vows, which I shall vow, be annulled' (Nedarim 23b). *Kol Nidrei* is a development of that statement.

KOL NIDREI: OBSERVATIONS

The *Kol Nidrei* text is a grammatical monstrosity. Composed in Aramaic, we seek absolution for vows that we made in the past from this Yom Kippur until next Yom Kippur.

There is a controversy in the Talmud about whether we seek absolution for rash vows of the past year or for the next year. In the eleventh century, Rabbi Meir, the son-in-law of Rashi, changed the text to read for the future year. Ashkenazic Jews follow his tradition, whereas Sephardic Jews retain the old interpretation.

Anti-Semites use this text as proof that the Jew is likely to break his promises and that his vows cannot be trusted. The Mishnah very clearly states that these are vows made to God in haste, and not promises and obligations to one's fellow man.

The origin of the *Kol Nidrei* melody is unknown, but undoubtedly ancient. It may be based on the Torah trope. There are also traces of the Gregorian chant. Its emotional appeal is overpowering.

Many rabbis oppose the recitation of *Kol Nidrei* as an easy means to avoid obligation. The Reform Movement omitted *Kol Nidrei* in the 1962 edition of Gates of Prayer.

The psychologist Theodor Reik, a Jew totally removed from his tradition, commented on the *Kol Nidrei*, "The *Kol Nidrei* speaks to the collective Jewish unconscious of his deepest tribal memories.

The Jew is uncomfortable with the word "sin." That salvation will be withheld because of sin is not a Jewish concept. The Bible states, "There is no man who does not sin." We are all guilty of selfishness, thoughtlessness, laziness, immorality, indifference.

There is a ḥasidic saying: "I prefer the *rasha'* (i.e., the wicked person) who admits that he is sinful to the *ẓaddik* (i.e., the righteous person) who knows that he is righteous."

FORGIVENESS

Rabbi Shlomo Riskin, Chief Rabbi of Efrat, writes, "The most significant . . . and awesome day of the Jewish year is Yom Kippur, our Day of Forgiveness, when even the most jaded and far-flung Jew wends his way to the synagogue and attempts a rapprochement with his traditions and his God."

Is it not strange that at the outset of this most poignant occasion, when the Holy Ark is opened and all the Torah Scrolls are revealed in their white splendor, the cantor leads a standing congregation in the *Kol Nidrei* prayer—a petition to nullify all vows and oaths! Would not a heartrending *Shema yisra'el* or *Avinu malkenu* be more appropriate?

Today's haunting, bittersweet melody for *Kol Nidrei* comes from the time of the Spanish Inquisition, when many Jews were forced to take a public oath of conversion to Christianity. Hence, the prayer took on a special meaning. Those oaths that had proclaimed loyalty to the Church were to be declared null and void. However, this is certainly not the origin of the prayer, since it is to found in the gaonic liturgy of the ninth and tenth centuries, six hundred years before Spanish persecution.

If we really wish to discover the significance of this prayer and of vows in general, we must take a deeper look at the subject of vows discussed in the Book of Numbers. (30: 3–11)

Despite their importance, Jewish law permits vows and oaths to be rescinded by two methods. The first is called abrogation (i.e., *hatarah*). If an individual did not understand how difficult it would be to fast, if it made him a nervous wreck and caused him to be short-tempered with his family, then such an oath can be abrogated by a Jewish court of three individuals. It is understood that indeed an oath had been taken, but that the individual was unaware at the time of its ramifications.

The second method is quite different. If the oath was made by a child or by a wife and is of a nature which will affect the relationship with her husband or father, then the parent or husband can rescind the oath as if it had never been made. This is called nullification (i.e., *hafarah*).

When the Day of Atonement arrives, all the things we should not have done but did or did not do but should have done parade before us. We seek forgiveness. We search for a precedent, a workable model, which exemplifies the possibility of canceling a committed action, of recalling a bitter word.

Our liturgy comes to our rescue. It reminds us, in the *Kol Nidrei* prayer, of the possibility of absolution. Therefore, just as three individuals can obliterate the implications of an oath because the one who made it may not have realized its implications, the Almighty can lift from us the responsibility of our wrongdoing because at the time of commission, we had lost sight of the full, eternal ramifications of our mortal actions. In Hebrew, it is called *kapparah*, or covering up.

What is unique about Yom Kippur is that it also allows us to see God in his role as Husband and Parent. Just as a husband has the power to obliterate the oath of his wife, or a father the oath of his child as if no oath had ever been made, so, too, does the Almighty—"husband" of the Jewish people and "father" of us all—have the power to erase our ill-advised words and unseemly acts against God as if they had never been committed. This is called *taharah*.

Yom Kippur is a day of profound love. Just as the husband or father who nullifies an oath does, so as an act of unconditional love in which they are willing to completely forgive and forget, Yom Kippur purifies us and washes away our sins in love as if they had never existed.

We often hear from those we love, "I can forgive, but I can never forget." To those individuals, the prayers of Yom Kippur reach out and say, "Those who truly love must not only forgive, but also forget."

Indeed, without such true forgiveness, no relationship can evolve. If a couple cannot forgive each other and honestly forgive past grievances, the marriage will end in divorce. If a father keeps reminding his child of past misdeeds or, for that matter, if a child keeps raising past mistakes with his parents, then both sides will brood about their imagined or real complaints, and end up worse than when they started out.

Why wait until Yom Kippur? Every Friday is a perfect day to forgive and forget. In so doing, you will take a big step toward making possible that wonderful peace which we call *shalom bayit*.

SHEMA: DECLARATION OF BELIEF

We do not pray the *Shema*. Rather it is called *Keri'at Shema*, or reciting the *Shema*. This prayer is a Bible lesson stating the basic principal of Judaism, the belief in monotheism. It is a tradition to prolong the last word *eḥad* (i.e., one) to emphasize the unity of God.

In many prayerbooks, the third letter of *Shema*, the *ayin*, and the last letter of the *Shema*, the *daled*, are elongated. The two letters together spell *ed* (i.e., witness). Abudarham taught, "This reminds us that every Jew's duty is to serve as a witness to God's unity."

Barukh shem is always recited silently during the year. However, on the Day of Atonement we recite this at the top of our voice. The custom may derive from Roman origins. When the Jew proclaimed his "praising the glorious kingdom" of God, it might have been seen as a challenge to the Roman Emperor. Therefore, the tradition arose to recite it silently. However, on the Day of Atonement, the Jew risked the wrath of the Romans and recited it aloud.

INTRODUCTION TO THE *AMIDAH*

The story is told that once, as an old *ḥasid* was sitting in his study praying, he felt a pain in his chest and saw his whole life passing before him. In the background, there was desert stretching to the horizon's edge and at every milestone of his life—his birth, his Bar Mitzvah, his wedding—he saw two sets of footprints in the sand, which he understood as his and God's.

However, at the tragic points of his life, sickness, the death of his parents, the drowning of his only son, the death of his wife, only one set of prints was visible.

Shading his eyes to look for signs of God's presence at these tragedies, he saw nothing, only one set of prints. Calling out to the Almighty he said, "Master of the Universe, where were you when I needed you most?"

The voice of the Lord rolled out of the desert, "Don't you remember? I was lifting you up and cradling you so that you could bear those moments."

PRAYER

Rabbi Naḥman of Kosov once said, "We should always have the Lord in our thoughts." The question was posed to him,

"Can we think of God when we are buying and selling?"

"Surely," he replied. "If we can think of business when we are praying, then we should be able to think of praying when we are doing business!"

PIYYUTIM

Some of our favorite prayers fall into the category of the *piyyut*, poetry that was added to enhance and embellish the service. The word poetry stems from the Greek. In Hebrew, the *paytan* composes a *piyyut*.

The medieval composers of *piyyutim* enriched Jewish literature, influenced the development of the Hebrew language, and even coined new words and phrases. The earliest example of poetic additions to the *mahzor* was composed in the sixth century. The liturgy was fixed. The *piyyut* was an effective means of self-expression. There are poetic contributions to the fixed liturgy of the *mahzor* composed in Spain, Germany, England, France, Poland, and Italy. The *piyyut* is the collective soul of the Jewish people. In many compositions, there are Arabic influences. Oftentimes, the poet would spell an acrostic of his own name. There are innumerable allusions to the Bible, Talmud, and Midrash. Also interspersed are laws of ethics and ritual. Often, when Jewish teachings were prohibited, *paytanim* translated them into poetry.

There are three separate periods in the creation of *piyyutim*: Judea—second to the eighth century (e.g., Yosi Ben Yosi, 6th century; Yanai, 7th century; and ha-Kalir, 8th century). North Africa—750 to 1250; we find the Muslim influence. Spain—tenth and eleventh centuries (e.g., Ibn Ezra, Ibn Gabriel, and ha-Levi.

Zunz was of the opinion that there were nine hundred composers of *piyyuttim*; Davidson raised the number to three thousand. Scholars say that 34,000 *piyyutim* were composed.

The function of a *piyyut* was to disguise thoughts and actions forbidden to discuss. The *piyyut* could allude to the problems of the Jewish people. These problems could not be stated openly. Easily memorized, the *piyyut* had a peculiar rhythm and acrostic sentences, which could easily be committed to memory.

Both Maimonides and Amram Gaon were opposed to the proliferation of *piyyutim*.

YA'ALEH TAHANUNENU, OR "MAY OUR SUPPLICATIONS RISE"

The author of this *piyyut* is unknown. Written as an inverted alphabetical acrostic, it is suggestive of the twenty-four-hours service of the Day of Atonement. We ask God that our prayers ascend at nightfall, arrive at His throne by dawn, and be answered at dusk.

Our problem is not affluence, but rather prometheanism, the idea that we are all powerful. The assertion of our power is a cover up of our insecurities. We pretend to be omnipotent and immortal. We build our little hideouts that will collapse in the first strong wind.

When we recite *Ya'aleh*, we do not seek material goods, but rather perspective that we can put our actions in the proper place. We are not all-powerful, but frail and finite. We appeal to the Divine forces from without for salvation.

We use the word *aliyah* (of the same root as *ya'aleh*), when one is called to the Torah, *aliyyah la-torah*. Settling in Israel is termed *aliyyah la-arez*. The Bible defines visiting the ancient temple in Jerusalem on the three pilgrimage festivals, *aliyyah le-regel*. At death, the term is *aliyyat neshamah*, the ascent of the soul.

SELAḤ NA, OR "FORGIVE, PLEASE"

Rabbi Meir of Rothenberg, the author of this *piyyut* and a leading German scholar, was confined by the bishop of his village to a prison fortress. His students offered money to ransom their revered sage.

Rabbi Meir refused lest he set a precedent, which would encourage ruthless bandits to kidnap rabbis and extort ransom money from his community.

He remained in prison until his dying day. Later, his body was brought to his disciples, who chose to be buried next to him when they passed away.

OMNAM KEN, OR "IT SURELY IS"

This *piyyut* is one of the few contributions in our *mahzor* from English Jewry. In 1290, the 16,000 Jews in England were expelled and not until the days of Oliver Cromwell and the Puritans in the seventeenth century, were they allowed to return.

In 1190, a mob recruited by Richard the Lionhearted assembled against the Jews of York. They withdrew to a castle and were given the choice of apostasy or death. Rabbi Yom Tov and sixty of his followers preferred suicide.

KI HINEI KAḤOMER BEYAD HA-YOẒER, OR "AS CLAY IN THE HAND OF THE POTTER"

In this *piyyut*, the author likens us to clay and God as the potter. At his pleasure and at his desire, he kneads us. We are like stone in the hands of the mason, we are like iron in the hands of the smith, we are like glass in the hands of the blower, we are like cloth in the hand of the wearer.

This is not blind fatalism, which is of Greek origin. Man has free will and God is not indifferent to our pleas. This *piyyut* expresses our dependence upon God and our plea for His mercy.

EL MELEKH YOSHEV AL KISE RAḤAMIM, "GOD, KING WHO SITS ON A THRONE OF MERCY"

This is one of the *seliḥot*.

The author I. L. Peretz tells the story of the *ẓaddik* of Nimirov.

The *ẓaddik* always absented himself from his synagogue on *seliḥot*. His *ḥasidim* explained that he "goes to heaven and intercedes on behalf of his congregation." The *mitnagdim* did not believe this and determined to follow him, certain that he was up to mischief.

They saw him take his ax and were certain that he was about to commit vandalism. They followed him to the forest and watched him chop down a tree. He brought the wood to an old, sick woman, who lived in a frail hut and lit a fire for her to provide warmth.

On the following *seliḥot*, the *ḥasidim* said, "Do you believe that the *ẓaddik* ascends to heaven on this night?" The *mitnagdim* replied, "If not even higher than heaven."

The purpose of the Day of Atonement is to commit to action and to noble deeds.

HAVIENU EL HAR KADSHI, "I WILL BRING ALL PEOPLE TO MY HOLY MOUNTAIN"

Judaism never postulated, "only my House is the true House." The Talmud states that the righteous of all nations shall have a share in the world to come.

Judaism believes that all religions have validity. Because of this outlook, we do not missionize or spend a penny a year to proselytize. We accept, however, the sincere convert with open arms.

SHEMA KOLENU, OR "HEAR OUR VOICE"

The prayer reads, "Hear our voice," not "hear our words."

S. Y. Agnon comments that in the Torah reading for Rosh ha-Shanah, God says to Abraham, *Shema bekolah*, listen to Sarah's voice, and you will do what she says. If Abraham will listen to her voice, he will realize how upset she is, will understand that the present situation is intolerable, and simply cannot continue. Ishmael cannot live in the same house with Isaac, nor can Hagar with Sarah. "Listen to her voice," not only to her words.

On Yom Kippur, we ask God to listen, not only to our words, but also to our voice. The words are not really ours; they are from a book, but the voice is ours. It expresses the hopes, the fears, the concerns we have. We pray that God will hear our voice and sense how great is our anguish, how deep is our need.

This is what it is like when we try to communicate with one another. It is not sufficient to listen to the words; we must also listen to the voice. We must catch the almost unexpressed cry for help, the barely articulated hint of distress, the nearly inaudible signal of anguish. It is not enough to give our children a good "talking to," Very often, what they crave much more is a good "listening to." We must hear their words, but even more, we need to listen to their voices.

SHEMA KOLENU

"Listen to our voice," Oh Lord, in gratitude for our many blessings—life, health, security, and family.

Most especially at *Kol Nidrei*, we ask God to hear our voices in gratitude for our beloved country. Never in history have Jews enjoyed as much security and so many opportunities to reach the highest pinnacles of success.

Jews are a bit more than two percent of the population of the United States. Yet ten percent of the Senate is Jewish, twenty-two percent of the Supreme Court and one quarter of the faculty of major universities in this country. There are Jews in the cabinet, heading the Federal Reserve, and NASA. Presidents of five Ivy League colleges are Jewish. Twenty-five percent of Nobel Prizes have been awarded to Jews. Jews are prominent in medicine, science, industry, finance, entertainment, the media, and every aspect of American life.

"Hear our voice" in gratitude, Oh Lord, and let us never take for granted the blessings that are vouchsafed to us by our beloved country. We are proud citizens of the United States, and may we continue to share in enhancing its growth and development. Devotion and commitment to the principles of democracy will enable us to continue to enjoy life, liberty, and the pursuit of happiness.

SHEMA KOLENU

"Hear our voice" stresses the vital importance of communication. Though this is a serious and sacred moment, the following story is appropriate.

A woman goes to a lawyer and tells him that she wants a divorce.

The lawyer asks, "Do you have grounds?"

She says, "About half an acre."

He says, "No, that's not what I meant. Do you have a grudge?"

She says, "No, we have a carport instead."

By this time, the lawyer is getting frustrated. He says to her, speaking very carefully, "Tell me, does he beat you up?"

She says, "No, I get up in the morning before he does."

By now, the lawyer has really had it. He says to her, "Will you please tell me exactly why you want a divorce?"

She answers, "Because he doesn't understand me!"

This humorous story illustrates that understanding one another is a most difficult task. On the High Holidays, we set aside ten days of prayer, study, talking, and listening. May we speak carefully and may we listen carefully. May we learn what God has to say to us and may we learn how to speak to God. May we listen to one another.

SHEMA KOLENU* AND *TESHUVAH

The story is told of a king who had an only son. He loved him dearly with all his heart and raised him to be righteous and to marry a proper wife.

Unfortunately, the son followed evil ways. He deserted his wife and associated with the wrong companions.

The king's love turned to hatred. He banished him from his kingdom to a faraway land.

His son wandered for many years. He was clothed in tatters and his face and visage had changed. Suddenly, he began to remember his father, and the love and support he had received at home. He yearned for his father and wanted to return and repent.

He did return and begged his father, the king, for mercy. He fell at his father's feet and beseeched forgiveness. He had changed so radically that his father did not even recognize him.

When his son cried out, the king remembered his son's voice and finally recognized him. The king restored him to the palace and opened his arms to his son in love and forgiveness.

The *nimshal* (i.e., lesson) is that God exalts us by giving us the Torah. When we turn aside from the Torah and follow evil ways, our very faces change. Now that the High Holidays have arrived, we regret our transgressions and seek to return to God. We cry out to God, *Shema kolenu*. If God will not recognize us, at least he will recognize our voice and spare us in compassion, accepting our prayer and gathering us to Him.

AL TASHLIKHENU LE'ET ZIKNAH, OR "DO NOT CAST US OFF IN OLD AGE"

Oftentimes, elderly parents weep openly when they chant this prayer. What is the reason?

It is the duty of parents to teach their children Torah, to develop their character, to bring them under the marriage canopy, and to ensure that they will perform good deeds. When a baby is born, we ask God that he bless the child with "Torah, *ḥuppah* (i.e., marriage), and *ma'asim tovim* (i.e., good deeds)."

On the other hand, the duty of children is *kibud av va'em* (i.e., honoring one's mother and father).

In old age, a parent looks forward to being comforted by the love and respect of his grown children, having fulfilled his duty towards them. The greatest fear of an elderly person is that his children in old age will cast him off. This will indicate the failure of his custodianship.

AL TASHLIKHENU LE'ET ZIKNAH

There is real pathos in the prayer *Al tashlikhenu le'et ziknah* (i.e., "Abandon Me Not in Old Age").

One of the innermost fears of the elderly is that they will live too long, some day become helpless and dependent upon others, be abandoned and forgotten. Their greatest fear is to be unwanted and unneeded, out of touch and a burden to others.

When we recite this prayer, we should remind ourselves not to abandon each other when those we know become old.

A rabbi once visited a nursing home, said nothing to any of the residents, nor did he tell them who he was. Rather he went to the piano, and played a familiar melody for them. People in wheelchairs gathered around the piano and joined in singing. Their eyes brightened and they became more alive.

We must reach out to others in their old age.

AL TASHLIKHENU LE'ET ZIKNAH: THE LITTLE BOY AND THE OLD MAN

(The poem by Shel Silverstein is a powerful commentary on "Cast Me Not off in My Old Age.")

> Said the little boy, "sometimes I drop my spoon,"
> Said the little old man, "I do that too."
> The little boy whispered, "I wet my pants."
> "I do that too," said the old man.
> Said the little boy, "I often cry."
> The old man nodded, "So do I."
> "But worst of all," said the boy, "it seems grown-ups don't pay attention to me.'"
> And he felt the warmth of a wrinkled old hand.
> "I know what you mean," said the old man.

KI ANU AMEKHA, OR "WE ARE YOUR PEOPLE"

"We are your people" and are obligated to conduct ourselves with pride, dignity, and self-respect on all occasions.

We can learn an important lesson from two great Jewish athletes of the past. In the 1930s, Hank Greenberg, first baseman of the Detroit Tigers, hit fifty-eight homeruns, two shy of Babe Ruth's record. In those days, there was no television, but the radio and the daily newspaper created great interest. He needed to hit two homeruns in five games. He was walked fourteen times on twenty-two occasions at bat. Rumor had it that anti-Semites did not want a Jewish ballplayer to hit more home runs than Babe Ruth. When he hit a grand slam in the ninth inning to win the pennant for Detroit, many cursed Hank Greenberg. In that year, he had 183 runs-batted-in. He was elected to the Hall of Fame, served overseas in the Second World War, having been one of the first ballplayers to enlist.

He was always proud and held his head high as a Jew. When he played in Detroit, it was during the Depression, the era of the anti-Semitic diatribes of Father Coughlin and the rise of Adolf Hitler.

It was two months before *Kristallnacht*. As a child, I will never forget that Greenberg was a few homeruns shy of the record. He asked his rabbi's advice about playing on Rosh ha-Shanah. The rabbi suggested that he attend services that morning and then go to the ball field. That afternoon, he hit two home runs. On Yom Kippur, he did not play. As a child, I could never forget the feeling of pride that surged through my breast.

The other Jewish athlete with dignity and self-respect was the pitcher Sandy Koufax. He refused to pitch for the Los Angeles Dodgers in the first game of the World Series because it was Yom Kippur. He won the seventh game and pitched two shutouts during that World Series.

I met Sandy Koufax when I served a congregation in Los Angeles. A most affable individual, he was not formally committed to Judaism. He explained to me that he realized he was a symbol and a role model to Jewish children everywhere. He abstained from playing on the Day of Atonement to set a standard.

None of us is a major-league ballplayer, but as parents, businesspeople, physicians, attorneys, we must set an example of pride and dignity for our children, clients, employees, and neighbors.

I am convinced that a non-Jew respects a Jew who respects himself. For we are Your people and You are our God.

THE ASHAMNU AND THE *AL ḤET*: THE CONFESSIONAL

Originally, there was one *Vidui* (i.e., confessional) at the beginning of Yom Kippur. In that way, the worshipper could begin the Day of Atonement free of sin. Later, many confessions were added. First, they were recited silently and then repeated by the cantor aloud.

In the Mishnah, Rabbi Yehudah urged us to specify each sin committed in exact terms. Rabbi Akiva, on the other hand, believed it should be a general confession.

The framework was the *Ashamnu*, which is the "lesser" confessional. Many verses were added in an acrostic manner. The *Al ḥet* is the "great confessional" and the form it takes is a double acrostic.

The confessional is not in the singular, but the plural, since everyone shares in the responsibility for the sins of society.

The emphasis of the sins confessed is one's relationship to others: misuse of words; irreverence for parents; disrespect for teachers; lack of business ethics; haughtiness and vanity.

The Talmud tells us, "Causeless hatred lead to the destruction of the Temple in Jerusalem."

"We have trespassed, we have dealt treacherously, we have robbed, we have spoken slander."

If we were to enumerate the occasions, from *seliḥot* to the end of Yom Kippur, when we publicly confess our sins in the traditional formulas of *Al ḥet* and *Ashamnu*, we would be truly amazed.

Vidui is most appropriate and significant for the Day of Atonement.

To whom do we confess our sins of commission and omission? Who listens? Who expiates and atones? Who grants us forgiveness?

Even for those who cannot believe in a Supernatural Being with whom we have this kind of dialogue, confession does have profound meaning for the penitent.

Long ago, Rabbi Samson Raphael Hirsch observed, "The *Vidui* ordained by the Torah does not consist of a confession to another person of sins; it is not even a confession made to God, but, as its grammatical reflexive *hitpa'el* form implies, it is a confession for which the sinner recalls to himself his sin."

In other words, the true import of confession is that it provides the mechanism wherewith the individual does not, or will not attempt to, conceal from himself his own past misdemeanors (What more does psychoanalysis profess to do?). Genuine confession must lead to some form of action during the Days of Awe. When we recite the *Al ḥet* and *Ashamnu*, we admit to ourselves that not only should we have acted differently, but that it was in our power to have acted differently. By doing this we admit to and proclaim our freedom of choice, and when we utter the formula, "I have sinned" in all sincerity, we include the idea, "I shall not repeat the offense" (Hirsch on Lev. 26:4).

When we say, "I have sinned," we must include the idea, "I shall not repeat the offense."

How does an individual know that his sin has been forgiven by Yom Kippur confession? Only by not repeating in the coming year the offense for which he today makes atonement.

The confessionals are in the plural to teach us when one sins it is as if the entire community is guilty. "All Israel are responsible, one for the other."

There is a story in the Talmud that a number of people were in a rowboat. One passenger began to drill under his seat and the water began to flood the craft. The passengers rebuked him, "How can you drill and allow the water to enter our boat. We will drown!"

He answered, "It is of no concern to you! I am drilling under my own seat."

We read in *Avot de-Rabbi Nathan*,

> "If you have done your fellow a little wrong, let it be in your eyes a great wrong. If you have done your neighbor much good, let it be little in your eyes. If your neighbor has done you a little good, consider it a great good. If he has done you a great wrong, let it be in your eyes insignificant."

There are three words for sin in Hebrew. *Ḥet* means to "miss the mark." *Avon* means "crooked," deeds of insolence. *Pesha'* means "rebellion" against God.

After each category of sins, we recite the three words of forgiveness. The first is *selaḥ*. It is an Akkadian cognate, from *s'alachu*, and means literally to be "sprinkled with water." In other words, this first word views forgiveness as a deodorant: the sin is intact and all we must do is add a little perfume so that the odor is not too pronounced.

The second word for forgiveness is *meḥal*. It means "to wipe out." We blot out our sin completely. However, we can never restore our pristine innocence. Therefore, forgiveness is more than "sprinkling," but it has to be something less than "blotting out."

The third and best word is *kapper*. It means "to cover over." We cannot pretend that we did not sin, nor should we constantly recall our sin, but rather we must cover over and begin again.

Kippur means atonement. A word derived from this is *kapparot*. In olden days, a chicken was taken on a string and wound around and around. The chicken was the scapegoat bearing the sins of the people. *Zo kapparati* (i.e., "This is my scapegoat"). We often wonder what the chicken was thinking seeing himself being whirled around. There is a Hebrew expression, *tarnegol kivnei adam* ("a chicken is like a man").

How often in life do we make others a convenient *kapparah*. For our own failings, we scapegoat a wife, a parent, an employer. We make a *kapparah* of the physician, the attorney, the accountant, the rabbi, or the governmental official.

Someone suggested that we should recite a confessional for feeling guilty about sins that others accuse us of.

A daughter criticizes, "You never come to see your grandchildren!"

A mother rebukes, "You never call or visit me!"

A husband exclaims, "You don't know how hard I work for you!"

A wife whines, "You don't care about me. You never tell me 'I love you.' "

A neighbor says, "You never say hello to me."

Perhaps there are times we should not feel guilty about the sins that others accuse us of.

Many find it hard to forgive, thinking that it is a sign of weakness.

I know a woman whose husband walked out on her ten years ago. She works two jobs and struggles to support the two little children he left behind.

"Rabbi, how can you ask me to forgive him for what he did to us?"

I replied, "What he did was unacceptable. It was truly selfish of him. However, you must forgive him because he has no right to live inside your head and to make your life miserable. He has no right to make you angry and bitter all these years. Rid yourself of him and stop thinking of yourself as a victim."

Simon Wiesenthal tells the story of a man in a DP camp who implored him to loan him $10, promising to pay him the following week. Each week he made another excuse. Finally, after many months the man said, "The money has arrived. Here is your $10."

Said Wiesenthal, "Keep it. For $10, I don't want to change my opinion of you."

Saadiah Gaon listed the stages of genuine repentance: renunciation of one's sin, remorse about one's transgression, request for forgiveness, and commitment not to relapse into the sin again.

AVINU MALKENU, OR "OUR FATHER, OUR KING"

Massekhet Ta'anit attributes the composition of this prayer to Rabbi Akiva in the second century, written during a time of draught. Originally, the words were abbreviated, "We have no King, but Thee." In time, more verses were added.

Katvenu be-sefer (i.e., inscribe us in the book) occurs five times in this prayer, and according to our rabbis, refers to the

Five Books of Moses. *Ḥayyim tovim* (i.e., good life) refers to the Book of Genesis, dealing with the creation of life. *Ge'ullah ve-yeshuah* (i.e., redemption and salvation) refers to the Book of Exodus, which records the salvation of the Jewish people. *Parnasah ve-kalkalah* (i.e., sustenance and support) refers to the Book of Leviticus dealing with sacrifices and festivals. *Zekhuyyot* (i.e., merit) refers to the Book of Numbers, which relates the merit of the twelve tribes in the wilderness. *Seliḥah* (i.e., forgiveness) refers to the Book of Deuteronomy, which expresses God's forgiveness.

We do not recite this prayer on the Sabbath. Prayers for relief from personal anxieties are inconsistent with the Sabbath. For this reason, the *Amidah* of nineteen daily prayers on the Sabbath retains only six, and one is added so that no personal petitions are part of the silent devotion.

Ki en banu ma'asim (i.e., "for we have no good deeds to plead our cause"). Surely, everyone has to his credit one good deed. A rabbi observed, "True, everybody has one good deed, but for this, he is deserving of only one moment of life and good health. Therefore, we do not have many deeds of merit."

The *maggid* of Dubno said that this is comparable to a man entering a store, putting many items aside for purchase until he reaches the cash register. Then, regretfully, he tells the cashier, "but I have no cash!" We ask God for life, health, prosperity, and security. However, we have no cash, no merit to deserve this. We have insufficient good deeds to our credit.

CHAPTER 5
YOM KIPPUR

THE SILENCE OF OUR SOULS

Rabbi Ismar Schorsch comments that to fast for a day is not what makes Yom Kippur difficult for us. Fasting gets easier with age. The challenge of Yom Kippur is to do without the distractions to which we are addicted. Ours is a society that abhors silence. We jog with earphones, run with music, fly with movies, and even entertain company with the television droning in the background.

In contrast, Yom Kippur asks us to take refuge in the silence of our inner selves. As the cacophony of distractions wanes, we begin to feel the yearnings of our repressed souls, "Like a hind crying for water, my soul cries for You, O God; my soul thirsts for God, the living God; O when will I come to appear before God?" (Ps. 42:2–3). We are more than our appetites and belongings, our ambitions and achievements. We also bear within us a touch of transcendence that has the power to sustain and ennoble us.

Without inwardness, our lives are stripped of true nobility. "What is the meaning of nobility?" Abraham Joshua Heschel asks.

> A person possessing nobility is one whose hidden wealth surpasses his outward wealth, whose hidden treasures exceed his obvious treasures, whose inner depth surpasses by far that which he reveals. Refinement is found only where inwardness is greater than outward appearance. The hidden is greater than the obvious, depth greater than breadth. Nobility is the redeemed quality which rises within the soul when it exchanges the transient for the permanent, the useful for the valuable.

The intensity of Heschel's piety is surely in order for us on Yom Kippur when we reach for eternity, not via the roar of a spaceship, but the reverberations of our souls. It is the speck of divinity that resides at the core of our being and strives to be restored to its ultimate source, the Source of All Being. In the eleventh century, the gifted Spanish Jewish poet and philosopher Solomon Ibn Gabirol, who died at age thirty-seven, called God in a striking formulation "the Soul of All Souls" (i.e., *neshama le-neshama*). The linkage is indelible and inextricable. The universal human quest for God is rooted in that spiritual patrimony.

The power of this conception of human life is that it makes us part of something infinitely greater than ourselves. For a fleeting moment, we become the vessel of a spark of pure spirit, like a light bulb turned on with the flick of a switch. The electricity that flows through the circuit existed before the light went on and will not vanish after it goes out. The bulb is not more than one tiny fragment of a vast system of industrial energy.

Every one of us carries a deposit of ultimate worth. To save our soul, not in the sense of eternal salvation but spiritual nourishment, is the prerequisite for saving the life of another human being. Oblivious to the affinity between the human and the divine in each of us, we would not lift a finger to improve the welfare of our neighbors, near or far. May the insight that comes from the observance of Yom Kippur inspire us to reach for loftier standards of piety and ethical behavior in the year to come.

WE WEAR DOWN OUR DEFENSES

Yom Kippur comes to wear down our defenses. We fast for twenty-four hours. We spend the entire day in prayer. We repeat confessionals repeatedly, "for the sin we have committed before You . . ." almost like an interrogator browbeating a witness, until finally, through a combination of physical and emotional weariness, we stop denying, we stop defending ourselves, we stop making excuses. We admit that we were weak, superficial, selfish, confused about what is important. The moment we do that, something unexpected happens. We do not feel humiliated, exposed, put down. We feel relieved, clean, and strong. All that energy we put into rationalizing and justifying ourselves can now be used to do other things.

WE MASQUERADE

The Kelmer Maggid, a great preacher, said, "Yom Kippur suggests Yom ki Purim." (i.e. "A day like Purim.")

What is the connection? On both days, it is customary to don masquerade or costumes. On Purim, Jews masquerade as *goyim*. On Yom Kippur, *goyim* masquerade as pious Jews.

KERI'AT HA-TORAH, OR TORAH READING FOR YOM KIPPUR

The Torah Reading of Leviticus 16 describes the ancient sacrifices that were brought to the Temple on the Day of Atonement. Two goats were selected by lot, one to serve as a sacrifice to the Lord. The other was called *azazel*, and it symbolized wickedness. The Priest confessed the sins of the people, and then sent the goat off into the wilderness. This is the origin of the word "scapegoat."

This rite recalls the desire of our ancestors for atonement. Crude and unsophisticated as it was, the principle is relevant. We seek atonement, purifications, and forgiveness. When the temple was destroyed, in its place was instituted the synagogue. Prayer replaced the sacrificial offering.

The Torah Reading was always the centerpiece of the service, preceded by *shaharit* and followed by *musaf*. The Torah Reading was supremely important in that God's word was to be studied by the people. Originally, the purpose of the Torah reading was to teach so that all could share of the knowledge of Torah.

On the Sabbath, seven are called to the Torah. On Yom Kippur, six; on festivals, five; on *Rosh Hodesh*, four; the Torah is also read very briefly on Monday and Thursday at which time three are called.

It is interesting that the origin of reading a short portion of the Torah on Monday and Thursday had to do with market day in Jerusalem. Many of the farmers lived far from the vicinity of a synagogue and consequently were unable to hear the Torah reading. However, on Monday and Thursday, they would bring their cattle and sheep to Jerusalem to the market and so it was instituted that the Torah be read briefly on the market days of Monday and Thursday so that all could share in the privilege of the study. In ancient days, everyone who was called to the Torah (*aliyah*) read his own portion. Later, a *ba'al koreh* read the Torah for everyone.

Aliyah means to ascend the platform, spiritually to elevate ourselves as we recite the blessing over the Torah.

The Torah is the possession of the entire congregation. In many traditional synagogues, the *bimah* (i.e., platform) is in the middle so that those in the congregation will surround the Torah. On a festival, we read the final portion from a second scroll. In actuality, we could read the section from the first scroll of the Torah, but it would be disrespectful to spend time rolling the Torah to find the proper passage.

HAFTARAH FOR YOM KIPPUR MORNING: THE MEANING OF THE FAST

The selection from the prophet Isaiah is most appropriate for this day of fasting. He condemns those who adhere to the form of fasting and yet violate its spirit.

From Isaiah we learn that fasting has a much higher meaning.

Why do we fast on the Day of Atonement? The answer cannot merely be that it is medically sound to rest our stomachs. Nor is Judaism a religion of asceticism in which we indulge in self-torture and self-flagellation.

There are four reasons for fasting. We create a spiritual mood. On this one day, we are urged to forget the desires of our body and concentrate on our souls. We also strengthen self-discipline. We must include the word "no" as part of our vocabulary! Tradition has it that there are 613 commandments, the majority of them, 365, are "thou shalt not." Negative commandments help us achieve self-discipline. We are not just machines. Self-control and self-mastery can improve our moral fiber. In addition, fasting helps us determine to live a better life. Finally, fasting arouses sympathy for our fellow man, many of whom do not have sufficient food every day of the year.

Today's Torah reading stresses ritual. However, the *haftarah* from Isaiah discusses ethics. Isaiah's teaching is that we must strive for the higher life, by helping the poor and the needy, by promoting justice and righteousness.

Is there really a dichotomy of ritual and ethics? The story is told of Rabbi Israel Salanter during a time of the plaque of cholera in Vilna. On Yom Kippur, he posted a notice on his synagogue door urging his congregation to sustain themselves with food and walk as much as possible. To emphasize his admonition, knowing that his congregation would not taste food on the Day of Atonement, he ate bread publicly on the pulpit on Yom Kippur. He exclaimed, "I do not think less of Yom Kippur, but more of the human being." This is the true spirit of Jewish law. The Sabbath was created for man and not man for the Sabbath. Jewish tradition teaches that if threatened with death, one can violate all but three of the commandments, idolatry, murder, and immorality.

TESHUVAH, OR "REPENTANCE"

The three As in the process of repentance are awareness; we must first admit that we have sinned; apology; it is not sufficient to apologize, but we must seek out those whom we have wronged and express our deepest regret. In olden times, the Jews, on the morning of *Kol Nidrei*, would visit the homes and shops seeking apology from people whom they wronged; anticipation; if the same circumstances were to arise during the coming year, we would not succumb to the same temptation.

VAHAVIENU LE-ZIYON IRKHA BE-RINAH, OR "LEAD US WITH JOY TO ZION, YOUR CITY"

The Jew never forgets his attachment to the Holy City of Jerusalem. We face east when we pray. One of the interpretations of breaking a glass at a wedding has to do with the destruction of the Temple. On Tishah be-Av, we fast and read Lamentations in commemoration of the destruction of both Temples. In the traditional home, there hangs a *mizrah* sign denoting the east. The devout Jew rises at midnight for *tikkun hazot*, mourning the destruction of Jerusalem. The *geshem* and *tal* prayers have to do with rain and summer dew falling in Israel.

Vahavienu can be sung to the music of *Ha-Tikvah*, the Zionist National Anthem. Nissim Belzer set this to music in 1860. The theme of the music was borrowed from the composer Smetana. Much later, the *Ha-Tikvah* was adopted as the national anthem of the Zionist Movement.

ALEINU: KNEELING

In the synagogues of old, the entire congregation would fall at *korim* during the *Aleinu* and the *Avodah*.

Today, they sit back politely and allow the rabbi and cantor to fall prostrate to the floor.

Why not encourage as many congregants as possible to fall in the aisle. Perhaps they might feel uncomfortable or embarrassed to bow and kneel to God. Modern man and woman assume that they are too sophisticated for such an ancient rite. Restoring the tradition might remind us that there is a God who rules the world and that we should leave many of the problems we cannot solve to God.

Sharon Strassfeld comments,

> When I was a teenager, I began reading serious philosophical works. I concluded that God did not rule the world, that in fact, God and we are partners. One Yom Kippur, in consonance with my new thinking, I decided not to "fall *korim*" for the *Aleinu* prayer. My *zaydee*, who had eagle eyes, even for the upstairs women's balcony, asked me to take a walk with him during the break in services. He wondered, he told me, why I hadn't "fallen *korim*." I explained that it was a *neue velt* (literally, a new world). *Zaydee* listened and then asked,

thoughtfully, "Sherelleh, tell me more about this *neue velt*." I did, telling him about all the things I had been reading and thinking.

When I finished, my grandfather said to me, "This new world you speak about I understand. But there is one thing I don't understand. In this new world, if you don't bow before God, before whom will you bow?"

That is a serious question, is it not? If you do not bow before God, before whom will you bow instead?

Will you bow before Mars, the god of war, or Venus, the god of beauty, or Mammon, the god of money? or will you worship your own ego? Your body? Your status? Your bankbook? Your flag? or yourself?

If not, consider *korim* instead. It is much safer and much wiser.

OḤILAH LA-EL

This is a note for the scholars in the congregation. On the Day of Atonement, the *Aleinu* is recited and then the *Oḥilah la-el*. However, on Rosh ha-Shanah, the order is reversed. First comes the *Oḥilah la-el* and then the *Aleinu*.

The explanation is that on Rosh ha-Shanah, the *Oḥilah la-el* introduces the *Malkhuyyot* (i.e., the King verses). The *Aleinu* is part of the *Malkhuyyot*.

On Yom Kippur, there are no *Malkhuyyot* and so the *Aleinu* stands by itself which is followed by the *Oḥilah la-el*, which introduces the *Avodah*.

AVODAH

The *Avodah* rehearses the elaborate Temple ritual that was performed by the High Priest on the Day of Atonement. This service describes in detail the procession, dress and sacrificial ritual. Since the destruction of the Temple, this *Avodah* was placed in the *musaf* in order to remember the systematic recapitulation of the ancient ceremony.

Avodah literally means "to work." In Israel, work and religion are often equated.

There is a famous passage in the Mishnah that the world "rests upon the Torah, *avodah*, and *gemilut ḥasadim*" (i.e., good deeds).

The word for sacrifice in Hebrew is *korban*: It is derived from the word to approach or "come near." When we offer material possessions and ourselves to God or to a cause, we are truly sacrificing in the ancient tradition. The ancient sacrificial system symbolizes our duty to dedicate ourselves in the service of God.

The ancient *Avodah* service contained all elements of holiness coming together; the holiest individual, the holiest time, and the holiest place.

ELEH EZKERAH VENAFSHI ALAI ESHPEKHAH, OR "THESE I RECALL, AND I POUR MY HEART OUT"

This is the occasion when we commemorate all of the martyrs who have died for *Kiddush ha-Shem*.

In this *piyyut* the question, "How was it possible for ten righteous men to have been executed with such horrible deaths?" is addressed.

This poem was composed in the eleventh century after the First Crusade. It reflects the bewilderment of the people that so many innocent martyrs could have been put to death. Our tradition states, "The soul that sinneth, it shall die." What kind of a God would permit the innocent to be punished?

This poem is a pathetic search for explanation. In 1100, the Jews of Mayence sought refuge in their synagogue from a frenzied mob.

Rather than renounce Judaism they were prepared to lose their lives. Others preferred to kill their own children and wives, and then themselves. This *piyyut* explains the tragedy without impugning the characters of the victims, without accusing God of abandonment.

The ten martyrs were executed not because of their own sins but because of the kidnapping of Joseph many centuries before. As the Ten Martyrs, so the Jews of Mayence were innocent of sin.

The historical background of this *piyyut* is set in 135 C.E., during the time of the Roman emperor Hadrian. The emperor, to find pretext for the persecution of great Jewish scholars, approached the rabbinic leaders and asked whom his brothers executed for the kidnapping of Joseph. Since no one paid the penalty of death, he determined that ten rabbis would be substituted for this unpunished crime. Rabbi Ishmael, the High Priest, ascended to heaven in order to determine that the sentence was to be executed.

Rabbi Ishmael exclaimed, "I will go first, because I cannot bear to see a great scholar put to death." However, Rabbi Simeon ben Gamaliel went first. Ishmael raises his colleague's severed head exclaiming, "How the tongue of Torah has been brought to the ground."

Rabbi Ishmael is next. The daughter of the emperor cried out, "Spare him for he is a handsome man." The Roman executioners flayed his skin. When they reached the portion of his arm where the *tefillin* are placed, the angels in heaven protested bitterly. A *bat kol*, a voice from Heaven, proclaimed, "One more objection and I will restore the world to *tohu va-vohu*!"

When Rabbi Akiva was executed, they ripped his flesh from his body. They wrapped Rabbi Hananiah ben Teradyon in the parchment of the Torah and placed wet wool on his heart to prolong the pain. Suddenly, the words of the parchment fly into heaven for eternity.

In this tragic vein, the poem continues.

Historically, the ten rabbis recorded in this *piyyut* did not live in the same generation and could not possibly have been executed together. Undoubtedly, this was the attempt of our sages to explain the martyrdom of innocent people.

AL ḤET SHEḤATANU, OR "FOR THE SIN WE COMMITTED"

There are forty-four sins enumerated in the *Al ḥet*. They do not deal with major crimes, such as murder, robbery, blasphemy, or idolatry. They do not contain any ritual violations, such as of dietary laws, the Sabbath, fasting, or prayer.

We have until Yom Kippur to repent. We are not righteous, nor are we without sin. We are not very wicked and beyond redemption. Rather, *teluim ve-omdim*. The wicked immediately are consigned to the netherworld. The righteous are immediately assigned to Heaven. Those of us "in the middle" have ten days to make atonement.

The *Al ḥet* is concerned with the sins of good people. These sins are not punished in courts of law. These sins are subtle and intangible. We do not confess to stealing, but rather "taking advantage of or cheating." We are not accused of beating our fathers, rather *zilzul*, holding parents in contempt. There are sins of personal morality: not robbery, but *harhor ha-lev*—sins of the heart; *sikkur ayin*—wanton looks; *zediyyat re'a'*—trapping one in a business transaction; and *tesumet yad*—breach of trust. Other sins mentioned in the *Al het* are *rekhilut*—slander; *lashon ha-ra'*—gossip; *dibur peh*—spoken words; and *tifshut peh*—distortion of words. Inner attitudes included are *immuz ha-lev*—hardening of the heart, bearing a grudge, and insensitivity; and *kasheyut oref*—stiff-neckedness, obstinacy and envy. Then there is the climax, *Hillul ha-Shem*—disgracing the name of God.

These are not major crimes perpetrated by master criminals. These are sins and transgressions of good people, but by no means minor.

THE *ASHAMNU* AND THE *AL ḤET*: THE CONFESSIONAL

These are the two confessionals in the Yom Kippur service. They each contain a category of sins. As we look at the list, we are tempted say that sin has not changed very much during the last many centuries.

A Protestant evangelist once announced a sermon titled "The Six Hundred and Seventy-Nine Sins." People were very curious and the church was filled to overflowing because many thought there might be a sin that they had overlooked.

Most of the sins that are listed are relevant; they are sins of commission or sins of omission. I remember in a past congregation, Uncle Ely, who was well into his nineties, after every service would approach me and say, "Rabbi, why do I have to recite this list of sins? I am too old to have committed them."

Our approach is if the sins exist in our community, then we are responsible. That is why all of the sins are recorded in the plural and not in the singular. If a sin exists in the community, we are guilty.

When we examine the list of sins, we see that they do not encompass major sins, murder, robbery, blasphemy, or idolatry. Most of these are sins of personal morality. They are not major crimes, but they are destructive of our personalities and corrosive of our characters.

Why are the sins listed alphabetically? This is a mnemonic device for a time when books were not printed. The rabbis also felt that if we listed the sins from the beginning of the alphabet until the end, we would have exhausted our vocabulary.

A rabbi was asked the question, "Why are these sins listed alphabetically? We do not sin alphabetically!" He answered that we must come to the end of the list of sins or we would remain in the synagogue the entire day.

YONAH, OR THE READING OF JONAH IN *MINḤAH* OF YOM KIPPUR

Why do we read the Book of Jonah on the Day of Atonement? This is not a "fish story"!

Jonah did not want the wicked city of Nineveh to be spared. He did not want to provide them the opportunity to do *teshuvah*. Unlike Jonah, on the Day of Atonement we pray for forgiveness, not only for ourselves but also for all people everywhere Yom Kippur teaches us that we cannot run away from our responsibilities. Jonah tried to avoid God's call to warn the people of Nineveh.

God forgives the repentant sinner. Oftentimes, insensitive and unsympathetic scholars utilize biblical criticism to express a higher form of anti-Semitism. One of their number said, "The Old Testament is devoid of universalism." Since the Book of Jonah is a protest against chauvinism, they term this "a later book of the Bible." Yeḥezkel Kaufmann believed that the Book of Jonah was written long before the Babylonian exile. Both Jonah and Ruth are Books that bespeak universalism.

The psychologist and author Abraham Maslow speaks of what he calls the "Jonah Complex," that is, "running away from one's own greatness." He elucidates his theme:

> It is certainly possible for most of us to be greater than we are in actuality. But we have a fear of our own greatness. We run away from our own best talent. We all have unused potentialities or not fully developed ones. It is certainly true that many of us evade potentially successful vocations so often we run away from the responsibilities dictated (or rather suggested) by nature, by fate, even sometimes by accident, just as Jonah tried in vain to run away from his fate.

Professor Nahum Sarna comments, "We read the Book of Jonah on Yom Kippur because the answer is clear. The major themes of the book are singularly appropriate to the occasion—sin and divine judgment, repentance and divine forgiveness."

What is remarkable is that the work is not at all about Israel. The sinners, the penitents, and the sympathetic characters are all pagans whereas the anti-hero, the one who misunderstands the true nature of God, is none other than the Hebrew prophet. He is the one whom God must teach a lesson in compassion.

It is precisely these aspects of the sublime prophetic allegory and particularly the sub-themes of the book that are appropriate for Yom Kippur. These motives attracted the ancient

Jewish sages and lead them to select Jonah as one of the day's two prophetic lectionaries: its universal outlook; its definition of sin as predominantly moral sin; its teaching of human responsibility and accountability; its apprehension that true repentance is determined by deeds and established by transformation of character (Jon. 3:10) not by the recitation of formulas, however fervent; its emphasis on the infinite preciousness of all living things in the sight of God (Jon. 4:10–11); and finally, its understanding of God as "compassionate and gracious, slow to anger, abounding in loving kindness" (Jon. 4:2)—all these noble ideas of the Book of Jonah constitute the fundamentals of Judaism and the quintessence of Yom Kippur.

CHAPTER 6
YIZKOR OF YOM KIPPUR

YIZKOR: THE EMPTY CHAIR

Yizkor on Yom Kippur is particularly meaningful and poignant. Always on Yom Kippur, we notice the empty places in the synagogue of those recently deceased. We feel the loss of those who are gone. The empty chair seems symbolic.

Artists have often used the empty chair theme to depict desolation, despair, and death.

Examples are Luke Filde's drawing "The Empty Chair," after the death of Charles Dickens, and Van Gogh's "The Empty Chair."

Another empty chair comes to mind, that of Reb Naḥman of Bratslav, who died in 1811. His chair stood empty in Uman. His disciples never elected a successor. The Soviets would not allow his chair out of country. During the Holocaust, the *ḥasidim* smuggled it out piece by piece. Finally, they reassembled it in the Bratslaver *shtiebel* in Jerusalem. That empty chair sits alone and unoccupied. However, it is not as empty, hopeless, or forlorn as you might think. Why not? Over the entrance to that *shtiebel* is a saying of Reb Naḥman, which has become an inspirational motto: *Gevalt Yidn! Seit sich nicht meyaish!* (i.e., "For heaven's sake, Jews, do not despair!").

This has been the motto of Jews through the ages! This should be our motto especially at *Yizkor* time.

INSCRIPTIONS FOR *YIZKOR*

In the Museum of the Diaspora in Tel-Aviv, in the entrance hall, there is the statement urging us "to remember the past, to live in the present, and to have faith in the future."

We must live in three dimensions. Unfortunately, some of us live in only one of these three dimensions.

There is another inscription in the Museum of the Diaspora in Tel-Aviv: "Would He really be God if he was worshipped just in one way?"

PARENTS AND CHILDREN

The Russian novelist Ivan Krylov tells the story of a wealthy pre-revolutionary family in Russia, sitting around the table in their elegant dining room enjoying sumptuous food. There are servants who feed them and they eat from expensive china. They sit there, the father and mother, the sons and daughters.

The grandfather, who has palsy, eats by himself in the kitchen. He is served his food on a wooden bowl lest he break the precious china.

The next day, the father went to work. When he returned, he discovered that his son had been whittling something from wood. He asked the child, "What have you whittled from wood?"

The son answered, "This is a wooden bowl."

The father replied "How wonderful, a wooden bowl for your grandfather."

"No." answered the son, "This bowl is for you when you are old."

It is not so much what parents say to their children, but the example that they set for them and the values that the children learn by observing their mothers and fathers.

A MOTHER'S TEARS

Ḥ. N. Bialik has an unforgettable description in his poem *Im yesh et nafshekhah la-da'at*, (i.e., "If you want to know").

The poet asks in his poem, "Do you want to know why there is a sigh in my heart and a tear in my eye when I recall my mother?" He describes his childhood as an orphan with many brothers and sisters. His poor mother works during the day in her inn and late at night, kneads the dough for her children's bread to sustain them in school. As she prepares her children's breakfast, she sobs and sighs. She asks God to help her in her struggles and hardships. Bialik listens to his mother complains to God. As she kneads the dough, tears fall down her cheeks and are mixed with the dough. In the morning, as the child eats he swallows the mother's tears.

"Now you know," says the poet why there is a sigh in my heart and a tear in my eye whenever I recall my mother."

HEARING YOUR NAME ON THE *YAHRZEIT* LIST

Even rabbis are prone to make mistakes every now and then. Of course, it is never the rabbi's fault.

One Sabbath, years ago, I read from the pulpit the names of our beloved departed from the *Yahrzeit* list of that week prepared by my secretary. Inadvertently, the office had listed the name of a living son instead of a departed father. The mistake could have had embarrassing consequences. However, the temple member who was there at services and heard his own name read before *Kaddish* reacted in an unusually sensitive and intelligent manner. I share with you in full his letter to me, without the name.

Dear Rabbi Silverman,

I attended last Saturday's enjoyable service. My reasons were twofold: the first to be with my children, and the second was to observe my father's *Yahrzeit*.

The temple office informed me of the dates and the bulletin had listed my father's name, Isadore. I attended with the expectation of hearing his name at the end of the service, but, much to my surprise, when you read your list, you named Paul (my own name).

My boys and I were dismayed; I almost missed saying *Kaddish*. I admit it was, spiritually, a shocking incident. As you can imagine, all kinds of thoughts ran through my mind. Standing with my children and hearing my name to be mourned at our temple made me suddenly think of the future. I would like to relate to you some of these thoughts:

First, I thought, when I am gone, will my boys actually respect the traditions of our religion and recite the *Kaddish* for me? Then I wondered if I shall have deserved the same love and respect as that shared between my father and me. Finally, I recalled that the *Kaddish* was originally recited in respect for learning and teachers. I realize now that my responsibility is not to command love and respect, but to teach my boys, stressing ethics, respect for others, moderation and preparation for life. Quite a job!

It is difficult to express these thoughts in writing, but please know that the impact was helpful and worthwhile.

So, thank you for the unintentional error. May all of our temple's administrative mistakes have such profound results.

> Sincerely,
> Paul

TWO BODIES OF WATER: RECEIVING AND GIVING

There are two seas in Israel, the Kinneret (i.e., the Sea of Galilee or Lake Tiberius) and the Dead Sea. The waters of the Kinneret are blue. They are very fresh. People swim in these waters. Fish are in abundance. There is great beauty when one gazes on this sea. On the other hand, the Dead Sea is located in the lowest spot in the world, 1000 feet below sea level. It has a tremendous salt content and is stagnant. There is a perpetual haze. There are no fish in the water, no sun overhead, no people live there. It is lifeless.

What is the reason for this? The source of the Kinneret is the river Jordan, which flows into the Kinneret and then flows from the Kinneret. The Kinneret, therefore, receives the pure waters of the Jordan and then gives them back.

The Dead Sea, however, has no outlet. The Dead Sea receives the water of the Jordan and then they become stagnant there.

Why? What is the difference between the Dead Sea and her vibrant sister, Kinneret, to the north? The Kinneret not only receives the life-giving waters, she freely shares them as well. The flow is continuous—it takes in, gives out, receives and shares—an organic flow of goodness, of loving abundance, of life energy. The Dead Sea is turned only toward itself. It receives, but it cannot give. A source to the north feeds it, but there is no sharing. Turned in upon only itself, the Dead Sea lives a hermit's existence, bringing precious little joy to others and feeling no joy itself. All take and no give has brought the Dead Sea to a form of spiritual suicide, a living death.

People are like these two seas. Some receive and transmit. Others only receive and never give back.

THE GIFTS THAT WE WITHHOLD

Rabbi David Wolpe comments on the book *Oliver Wiswell* by Kenneth Roberts. He has his hero reflecting remorsefully on the gifts he withheld from his father during his lifetime:

> In my mind there were thoughts of a thousand things I could have done for my father and hadn't. Ah!—and the thoughts of the things I hadn't said to him! Never once had I told him how I admired him, loved him. My whole life seemed to have been spent in taking all from him and giving nothing. Why hadn't I once—just once—told him what I so deeply and truly knew him to be—the best and wisest man in the world? No such word had ever come from me.

How many of us can read Oliver Wiswell's thoughts without a painful stab of recognition? Those of us who are too often involved in human grief can attest to the hash truth Harriet Beecher Stowe laid bare when she wrote, "The bitterest tears shed over graves are for words left unsaid and deeds left undone."

"Do not rob the poor, for he is poor." We are all poor, humble beggars, holding our tin cups for the precious coins of gratitude, affection, recognition.

We are all rich, fabulously rich. We have such precious gifts to bestow. A word of praise so many long to hear, a gesture of encouragement to lighten one's heavy burdens, an hour to listen to a loved one with our whole being, an act of forgiveness to repair a family breach, a thoughtful deed to banish loneliness and to brighten a dreary day.

Let us bring gifts now. We do not know how soon it will be too late.

The wonderful thing about bringing these gifts is that they not only enlarge the lives of others, but also our own.

The ultimate paradox is that when we stop robbing the poor, we start enriching ourselves.

CHAPTER 7
NE'ILAH

NE'ILAH, OR "CLOSING"

Ne'ilah is the last of the five services of the Day of Atonement: *Kol Nidrei, shaḥarit, musaf, minḥah,* and this fifth and final service, *Ne'ilah.*

Ne'ilah means "closing," and refers to the closing of the gates of the Temple and the closing of the book that was opened on Rosh ha-Shanah. There is no longer sufficient time to ask God to "inscribe us in the book of life," but rather we plea hot menu, "seal" us in the Book of Life.

One of the memorable prayers in the Ne'ilah service is *Petaḥ lanu* (i.e., "Open up the Gates"), for the day declines rapidly.

There is a special melody for the *Ne'ilah Kaddish* and *Avot.* In the mood of *Ne'ilah,* the melody is sad and plaintive. We are exhausted and this is our last chance for our prayers to reach the heavens.

Why do some people stand for *Ne'ilah*? The tradition of old was to open the Ark for the entire service, and for that reason people remained on their feet. In congregations where the Ark does not remain open for the service, there is little reason for standing. Our religion is not ascetic in nature; this is not the occasion to seek self-affliction and punishment.

Rabbis are tempted to announce at the end of *Ne'ilah* what time Rosh ha-Shanah services will begin the following year.

There is an ancient synagogue in Krakow. Few Jews are able to gather for Sabbath services. Mrs. Jacobowitz, the wife of the deceased *shamash*, is in charge of all arrangements in the synagogue.

A group of rabbis visited the synagogue on a UJA rabbinic tour. They asked her, "What can we do for the few Jews remaining in Krakow? Do you need money or clothing?"

"No," she replied. "Just remember us. Do not forget us. We are at *Ne'ilah* time in our community."

We are assembled in the synagogue today for *Ne'ilah*. However, the Jewish community of Krakow is really at *Ne'ilah* in its history. We have a year to which to look forward. They do not!

There is a *mahaloket* (i.e., controversy) in our tradition. Does the closing of the gate refer to the Gates of Heaven or to the gates of the Temple? The Gates of Heaven would be a better answer, for ours is a theology of the spirit.

The *Ne'ilah* service contains poetry of unusual beauty, melodies of great spiritual depth. There is a sense of urgency; there is no longer time to pray at length.

"Open up the gate . . . for the day declines rapidly."

The sun is setting and the lengthening shadows of night will soon bring on the darkness. We sense a physical weariness. However, as the initial pangs of hunger subside, we feel a renewed surge of spiritual strength and elation.

During these moments of lingering sadness, we exist in another sphere now ending. Soon we prepare for a return to the world. We began *Kol Nidrei* emotionally and powerfully, and now we end the Day of Atonement with a powerful statement.

PETAH LANU SHA'AR, OR "OPEN FOR US THE GATE"

Fasting and praying the whole day, we know that there is just one more hour for our prayer to reach the Gates of Heaven. As the setting sun filters its rays through the stained glass windows, even the music is weary and exhausted. Soon God's Book will close; soon the Gates of Heaven will be shut.

At this moment, we pray, "Open for us the gate—at the hour of the closing of the gate."

Many doors close upon us. There are the doors of death, when a beloved and precious member of our family is removed from our midst. Once the door of death is bolted shut on a precious life, we are left with our loneliness, yearning, and emptiness.

But then again, there are doors of life that close upon us, less dramatically, less conspicuously, but no less emphatically. In life, there is a constant closing of doors; graduation from college, going to war, marriage, children, entering a new business, moving into a new home. The closing of these doors always have an emotional effect upon us.

Doors also close in life upon our physical capacities—an accident, disability, or old age. We take for granted actions that were normal and automatic of which we were hardly aware—feeding ourselves, shaving, or driving a car. Now they may be out-of-bounds.

This prayer teaches us that we must accept gracefully the closing of doors, doors of death, and doors of life. We cannot pretend that these doors are still open. Once they are shut, we must proceed with life graciously. This is the measure of our growth and our maturity.

There is another message in the prayer. When one door closes, another door opens. God never closes one door without opening another door. We have all experienced in life, in our personal relationships with family, community, or in business a setback, a disappointment, or a tragedy. When the door closed upon us, we were certain that we could never, never make it. Somehow, we managed to see a new door, opening up for us.

They do me wrong who say I come no more,
When once I knock and fail to find you in.
For every day I stand outside your door,
And bid you wake and rise and fight to win.
Weep not for precious chances passed away,
Weep not for golden ages on the wane.
Each night I burn the records of the day,
At sunrise every soul is born again.

SHEMA AND THE FINAL SOUNDING OF THE *SHOFAR*

We begin the Day of Atonement with the emotional power of the *Kol Nidrei* prayer. Therefore, too, we must end our twenty-four-hour experience with a powerful confession of faith.

At the end of the *Ne'ilah*, we recite the *Shema* one time signifying, our belief in the one God. Then three times, we recite *Barukh shem* (i.e., "Blessed be the Name"). We complete this by reciting seven times, *Adonai hu ha-elohim* (i.e., "The Lord is God").

In *Mahzor Vitry*, we are told that God now ascends through the seven heavens and we accompany God.

The interpretation of singing the *Shema* one time indicates that there is not more than one God. Three times we recite *Barukh shem*, which brings to mind the three patriarchs, Abraham, Isaac and Jacob, the *Kol Nidrei*, which is recited three times, and the tripartite blessing of the High Priest.

We then sound the *shofar*, which in ancient times announced the jubilee.

SHOPPING IN A SUPERMARKET

It is possible to spend hours in the supermarket, going up and down the aisles, without interference. One can take from the shelves whatever one desires. However, eventually, the time comes when one stops at the checkout counter to pay for whatever was taken.

As the year ends, we enter into the High Holidays to give an accounting of our deeds during the past year.

LE-SHANAH HA-BA'AH BI-YIRUSHALAYIM, OR "NEXT YEAR IN JERUSALEM"

"Next Year in Jerusalem" is the call we proclaim at the end of Yom Kippur prayers, just as it is sung at the end of the Passover *seder*. On one day, we fast; on the other, we feast. How fitting that the Jewish people's physical and spiritual redemption is commemorated with the same prayer, directed to Jerusalem.

The government of Israel stands committed to protecting and preserving Jerusalem as the eternal, undivided capital of Israel and of all the Jewish people.

The traditional High Holiday liturgy contains the prayer, "May God grant happiness to His land and joy to His city. . . . The righteous shall rejoice . . . and all wickedness vanish like smoke." May this next year bring peace, unity, health, and prosperity.

A THOUGHT FOR NEXT YEAR

We are overwhelmed by the Yom Kippur experience. It is a unique twenty-four hours, replete with fasting, prayer, and meditation. When we complete the fast, we find that we have a "spiritual buzz" going. Spiritually, we are very high! It is a feeling of purification, cleansing . . . a catharsis.

Then comes the inevitable "letdown." How long will this spiritual mood continue? Two days, maybe a week, and then it is past! We want to know how to retain this spiritual mood.

Perhaps it would be wise to schedule Yom Kippur services once a month.

We assure ourselves that next year will be different. We will spend precious time with our family, our synagogue, and our priorities. The problem is that for many Jews Yom Kippur is "instant Lent." There are "revolving door Jews," in on Rosh ha-Shanah and out on Yom Kippur. There are three categories of Jews: drop-in, drop-out, and drop-off. We drop in on celebrations, a holiday, or Bar Mitzvah. As soon as our child is Bar or Bat Mitzvah, we drop out. Then again, many of us just drop off our children for religious school and then speed merrily on our way to our secular pursuits. There are cardiac Jews who never attend and never give but feel Jewish in their hearts. There are gastronomic Jews, whose only attachment is their love of Jewish food. There are alimony Jews, who are willing to pay dues and make pledges but have no contact or relationship. There are also agricultural Jews, whose Jewish participation is *in dred*—in the ground.

Now is the moment, as we leave the Yom Kippur experience, to pledge that we will take our religion seriously. I know an attorney who says to me every year after services, "I enjoy Yom Kippur so much. I feel relaxed; I am able to think. I realize how much I miss the synagogue during the year." Why cannot this be for him, and for us, a weekly experience? The synagogue offers Sabbath services, prayer, study, music, fellowship, and dialogue. The synagogue can inspire us and revolutionize our lives, add a dimension of meaning and value and beauty to each of us. Now is the time to pledge attendance at services, to enroll in a class, to study, to participate.